Preventative Legal Care

A Practitioner's Guide to Medical-Legal Fitness

Kevin W. Yankowsky

International Standard Book Number: 978-1-930536-77-7

Best Publishing Company
631 US Highway 1, Suite 307
North Palm Beach, FL 33408

Preventative Legal Care

A Practitioner's Guide to Medical-Legal Fitness

CONTENTS

INTRODUCTION

I have spent my entire professional career as an attorney working with and for the healthcare industry. For over 20 years virtually all of my clients have either been individual healthcare practitioners (physicians, nurses, nurse practitioners, etc.) or healthcare institutions (acute care hospitals, medical schools, long-term care facilities, pharmaceutical companies, etc.). During my two decades of practice I have performed essentially one role for my healthcare clients: I have defended them from allegations and attacks brought either in the civil justice system or in the regulatory realm. My health litigation defense practice covers virtually the entire gamut of adversarial legal disputes healthcare practitioners can face in this country, from commercial litigation to professional liability disputes to products liability claims. It also includes credentialing and medical peer review actions and industry specific regulatory disputes centered on statutes such HIPAA, HITECH, and EMTALA, among others. I have had the privilege and the pleasure of working directly with practitioners and healthcare officials as varied as world renowned surgeons and bedside nurses, international healthcare executives and administrators of small rural hospitals.

Throughout the course of my career I have gained some knowledge of how healthcare practitioners approach the medical and clinical aspects of their profession, probably just enough to be dangerous to myself and others. I have also gained a great deal of knowledge regarding how individuals and institutions in the healthcare arena view and approach the legal issues in which I specialize; specifically the identification and management of legal risk and the handling of legal disputes which often arise from it.

In September 2009 I had the opportunity to make a minor presentation at a major healthcare-industry conference in Washington, D.C. The keynote speaker at that event was the Hon. Thomas Daschle, former United States senator from South Dakota. I recall little of what I said during my small contribution to the program. However, something Senator Daschle shared with the audience has stayed with me to this day.

In general terms, Sen. Daschle spoke about the systemic healthcare problems facing the United States at the end of the first decade of the 21st century. He spoke eloquently and in great detail about a number of these important issues. During his remarks, he made one observation that I found particularly profound and enlightening.

A great deal of the problems facing healthcare in America can be traced to the fact that, as an industry, healthcare is an inverted pyramid in terms of priorities and resource allocation, Sen. Daschle told the audience. Since the days of the pharaohs mankind has known that a pyramid in its traditional form is one of the most stable and symmetrical building designs. Invert that near-perfect design, however, and you get a structure that can endure only as an artist's drawing.

In any logical society the base of the healthcare pyramid, in terms of both priorities and resources, should be medical prevention in all its forms, according to Sen. Daschle. Only after a broad-based foundation of preventative care has been established should the pyramid grow to include resources committed to other healthcare needs. Finally, only the very tip of the pyramid should represent resources devoted to acute end-of-life care.

Instead, as Sen. Daschle explained, the vast majority of healthcare resources in this country, the bricks that should form the preventative-care base of the pyramid, are instead directed to end-of-life acute-care issues. Similarly, only the tiniest sliver of resources, those sufficient to form only the very tip of a pyramid, are actually devoted to prevention. He concluded by opining that this inverted pyramid of resource allocation has distorted our healthcare system, preventing it from accomplishing many of the goals we as a society should want it to achieve.

When Sen. Daschle shared those thoughts he directed them primarily to an audience of physicians, healthcare executives, and other industry leaders. As I recall, I was one of the only, if not the only, practicing healthcare attorney in the audience. Perhaps for that reason his remarks struck me in a way he may not have intended.

What occurred to me that afternoon as I listened to Sen. Daschle's remarks was how well they described not only the allocation of clinical healthcare resources but also the healthcare industry's approach to the legal aspects of healthcare. In more than 20 years of private legal practice, I have represented individual clinicians and healthcare institutions involved in legal disputes of all shapes and sizes. Reflecting on Sen. Daschle's words, it occurred to me that, from a medical-legal perspective as well, prevention should be the primary focus of healthcare resource allocation. The broad base of the pyramid of resources devoted to medical-legal issues should be directed toward prevention. Only the smallest sliver of resources, at least ideally, should be devoted to the costly proposition of bringing medical-legal disputes to their final resolution. Or put in another way, only the smallest sliver of resources should be devoted to medical-legal end-of-life care. But, in my professional experience, this ideal allocation of resources is almost never found in the real world.

Time and time again I see healthcare providers and institutions expending immense sums of money (to say nothing of time and attention) to resolve legal disputes that potentially could have been avoided. These include disputes not only with patients but also with others in the healthcare industry, as well as the vast number of government agencies intimately involved in the healthcare system. While they willingly pay for settlements and aggressive legal defenses, so many people and institutions in healthcare either refuse or simply fail to invest a serious commitment of time, effort, and resources on medical-legal prevention. Instead they allocate their legal resources in the same inverted-pyramid shape in which society has allowed clinical resources to be funneled for so long and to such great detriment.

For this reason, after hearing Sen. Daschle's pyramid analogy I paid it the highest and most sincere form of flattery: I plagiarized it repeatedly. I did so because I believe it is a lesson that the vast majority of healthcare providers still need to hear. In a real sense, and in a great irony as well, healthcare practitioners in this country are guilty of the same cardinal sin with respect to their legal care that they rightly accuse so many of us layman with respect to our personal medical care. For years if not decades the healthcare community in this country has begged, pleaded, and sometimes even lectured ordinary Americans about their refusal to commit a bare minimum of time, effort, and resources to their own preventative medical care. Over the past several years I have challenged healthcare providers across this country to take some of their own medicine and finally agree to voluntarily commit some time, effort, and resources toward preventative care for their legal needs.

After speaking on this subject at industry conferences across the country for more than five years, I decided to try to condense many of the suggestions I have made in a variety of forums into a single volume. It is my hope that this volume might prove useful to a wide variety of decision makers in healthcare, from bedside nurses to independent physicians to healthcare executives in a variety of settings.

It is further my hope that the title of the book, *Preventative Legal Care*, is accurate. In the pages that follow I hope all healthcare industry readers find suggestions that they can apply to their healthcare practice to prospectively manage and minimize legal risks, legal complications, and, perhaps most important, legal expenses. And I hope they can do so in a cost-effective way, one that adds value to their practices. I absolutely insist that all of the suggestions and concepts in this book be completely consistent with the primary goal of every healthcare provider: to provide the highest quality and most consistently excellent care to his or her patients that he or she possibly can, every time, all the time.

Along those lines, let me note one important thing upfront: Nothing in this book is intended to be a road map to allow healthcare providers to avoid the just and appropriate legal consequences of the provision of poor-quality healthcare services or, still worse, illegal activity. This text is not designed to be a defense lawyer's handbook on how to "weasel out of" clinical or nonclinical mistakes. Healthcare providers who provide substandard care should always bear the legitimate legal and societal consequences resulting from that substandard care, including but not necessarily limited to the burden of compensation for any legitimate injuries or damages to their patients. Similarly, healthcare providers who intentionally or negligently run afoul of state and federal laws governing either the clinical or nonclinical aspects of their practice should fully expect to face and accept the regulatory and, in some cases, criminal consequences of those actions. Nothing in this book is intended to change or challenge those truths.

What this book is designed to do is to help healthcare practitioners recognize how their medical-legal risks are often uncoupled from both the quality of the care they provide to their patients and the diligence they apply toward professional compliance. After identifying some of the separate factors that lead to medical-legal risk unassociated with clinical care, this book is intended to supply practical, proven, real-world solutions to recognize, control, and in most cases minimize, if not totally eliminate, those extraneous but important medical-legal risk factors. It is my fervent hope that regardless of the nature of your healthcare practice, this book accomplishes these goals for you and that you enjoy reading it at least half as much as I enjoyed writing it.

CHAPTER 1

From Patient to Plaintiff

To completely understand and effectively manage the legal risks that accompany any healthcare practice, it is important to first recognize how those risks typically develop. For many, if not most, healthcare practitioners, professional healthcare liability remains at or near the top of legal risks associated with their practice. While more than a decade of nationwide tort reform may have diminished the severity of this risk, it has not, in my experience at least, eliminated it anywhere in the country. To state the obvious, the most effective way for healthcare practitioners to manage the legal risks associated with their provision of clinical care to their patients is to eliminate those risks to the greatest extent possible. And the most effective way to eliminate those risks is to minimize the number of patients who ultimately decide to become plaintiffs in the civil litigation system.

Let me make an important statement upfront: The single best and most important way to prevent your patients from becoming plaintiffs is to provide them with the highest quality care in every respect, at all times. Certainly, patients who receive negligent or substandard care have a significant probability of becoming civil-litigation plaintiffs. More important, they have an absolute right to do so. Every healthcare provider should both recognize and respect this right as well.

This text is not intended to dispute or attack the right of any person who has received substandard medical care to seek redress from the civil-justice system and recover all damages he or she may be entitled to under the law. Likewise, this text is not intended to be some type of "sneaky defense-lawyer road map" for incompetent healthcare practitioners who wish to avoid the justified legal consequences of providing truly negligent care to patients. Instead, I will address what seems to be a profound lack of understanding among both individual and institutional healthcare providers regarding how certain patients become civil plaintiffs. This misunderstanding, in my experience, is especially acute in circumstances in which a patient received care that was either arguably — or in some cases unquestionably — competent, caring and wholly within applicable legal and medical standards.

The question of how patients become plaintiffs is a good place to apply Occam's razor — the philosophical principle that, when in doubt, the simplest explanation is most likely the correct one. In this case, it is accurate to simply say that patients become plaintiffs when they: a) decide to seek out a plaintiff's lawyer and b) are then accepted by a plaintiff's lawyer as a client. As obvious as this statement may seem, it continues to amaze me how many healthcare practitioners go about their daily business without appreciating these simple but important truisms.

Furthermore, I have often found that there is a common misperception among healthcare providers regarding why individual patients seek out plaintiff's attorneys. Many practitioners paint this topic with a very broad brush, declaring that all such patients are motivated by the desire for financial gain (or as some have less politely put it, simply greed). In my experience, this is far from the truth. Certainly, some healthcare-liability plaintiffs, like some people in the general population, are motivated by a desire for the type of low-risk financial gain that critics of the civil litigation system often think it promises everyone. However, in over 20 years of experience it has been my observation that greed, while sometimes a contributing factor, is rarely the key motivator behind a patient's decision to seek a lawyer.

"The single greatest motivating factor behind a patient's decision to seek out a lawyer is most often a search for answers."

Instead, my professional experience has shown me that the single greatest motivating factor behind a patient's decision to seek out a lawyer is most often a search for answers. One thing that virtually all patients who seek lawyers have in common is that they have sustained a less than ideal result from their interaction with the healthcare system. By "less than ideal result" I mean that either they or their family member did not make the type of complete and uncomplicated medical recovery that, at one subconscious level or another, we all seem to expect every time we enter into the healthcare system.

Healthcare practitioners understand that complete and optimal recoveries simply are not medically achievable in every case. However, most patients do not approach the question of full recovery with the same scientifically objective viewpoint taken by practitioners. Whether based on facts, faith or hope, almost all patients, at one level or another, expect a full and complete recovery for themselves or their loved one. For this reason, any time a less than optimal recovery takes place in the healthcare system, it is natural for the patient to want to know why that occurred.

After years or even decades of liability exposure, healthcare professionals still do an extremely poor job of explaining to their patients how and why suboptimal outcomes occur. When questions regarding these types of outcomes are not answered by healthcare professionals, they will invariably be answered by someone else. These are not the types of questions that simply go away if ignored. For example, if someone seeks information about why his or her mother died of a post-surgical infection, it is extremely unlikely that person will forget about that question without receiving a satisfying answer. If the healthcare practitioners involved in the surgery do not answer the question, the next likely source of information will be the patient's family and friends, who in turn often suggest seeking the advice of an attorney. Once that suggestion is planted in the mind of a patient or loved one who has struggled to understand the reasons behind a medical complication or suboptimal result, it often takes root. In most cases, after a patient consults with an attorney, it is too late for medical practitioners to effectively change the ultimate conclusions that the patient will form about the care received.

Some healthcare practitioners answer questions particularly poorly after the completion of a healthcare procedure. Far too often the clinical specialist has moved on in his or her mind — as well as on his or her calendar — to the next patient and procedure. Even when a procedure has been completed without complication, this is a grave error, in my opinion. Simply put, the medical success of a procedure, while necessary for patient satisfaction, is sometimes not sufficient to generate that satisfaction. This is especially true in cases in which the post-procedure recovery of the patient is either long and/or physically or mentally difficult.

Far too often physicians and other healthcare practitioners simply assume that, because they know a procedure was a success, the patient should automatically recognize and fully appreciate that success as well. Practitioners who operate under this misconception often feel they have done their duty with respect to post-procedure communication with little more than a cursory visit and a statement as simple as "the procedure went well" or "you're going to be fine." They fail to recognize that their patient, who may indeed be fine, may not feel as well as he or she anticipated after the procedure was completed. That expectation, however unjustified it may be from a factual standpoint, can lead to dissatisfaction if not addressed through careful and detailed post-procedure communication.

This problem has increased exponentially in the 21st century, as the Internet and other means of rapid and almost effortless dissemination of medical information (not all of it accurate) has given every patient the opportunity to feel like an expert on medical issues, even if he or she is far from one. In our modern world, vast numbers of patients utilize the Internet and other easily accessible sources of information to learn not only about their practitioners themselves, but also about their underlying medical conditions and the procedures they are scheduled to undergo. What this means for practitioners is that a significant percentage of their patients have what they feel to be an educated and accurate understanding of complicated medical issues even before their medical treatment is provided. When a patient who has done this type of pre-care research receives the type of paltry communication described above, the disconnect between patient expectation and patient experience is often profound. It can and does often lead to medical legal complications which might otherwise have been avoided.

This inherent problem is even more serious in circumstances in which a less than ideal medical outcome has occurred, regardless of whether it happened as the result of an unforeseen and unavoidable complication or the result of questionable care. In some cases perhaps a sense of embarrassment about the complication or unfortunate outcome may play a role in the reticence of some healthcare providers at this critical stage of the medical-legal process. For whatever reason, during the critical hours and days after a patient first learns of an adverse outcome, the person most capable of accurately and effectively answering the unavoidable questions about what happened — the practitioner — often cannot be found, leaving the patient with little choice in many scenarios but to seek the counsel of family or well-intended friends, which often leads to a recommendation to seek the counsel of lawyers.

Simply put, as medical practitioners strive harder to obtain and identify medically acceptable patient outcomes, they often lose sight of the important goal of achieving overall patient satisfaction. Successful medical procedures are some protection against medical-legal risk. Satisfied patients are almost a guaranteed way to eliminate it.

Aside from the availability of communication in the healthcare setting, another equally important problem is the accuracy of the communication that does occur. Certainly, the failure to provide answers when needed can lead patients to seek outside counsel. However, inaccurate or otherwise inappropriate answers can also have the same affect.

In my own practice I have often been amazed to learn during the course of litigation that a patient decided to seek legal counsel because of an inappropriately negative comment made by one of the patient's other healthcare providers about the care received. In some cases, hostility between healthcare providers leads to this unfortunate occurrence. This is sometimes the case with nonphysician clinical providers who bear animosity toward certain physicians. As the universally perceived, if not legally responsible, "captain of the ship" with respect to every patient, every physician should recognize the importance of maintaining good, professional relationships with all subordinate practitioners involved in his or her practice. It often takes only one critical subordinate making an off-hand comment to damage the crucial trust associated within a physician-patient relationship. Diminished trust coupled with poor physician-patient communication can direct a patient's search for answers in an unfortunate direction from a medical-legal standpoint.

But more common than simple animosity is, in my judgment, a misguided desire to be overly helpful. Time and time again I hear about lower-level practitioners attempting to explain complicated medical procedures and situations to patients far above and beyond their own level of medical training and expertise. Often this is done out of an entirely altruistic desire to help the patient understand a difficult and confusing situation. Sometimes it is done out of perceived necessity because the more highly medically trained professional who should be answering those questions is not available. Regardless of the motivation, an imprecise or inaccurate answer to a complicated medical question often creates more confusion and uncertainty than it solves. And the more confusion or uncertainty that exists in a patient's mind, the more likely that patient is to seek answers from a third party, potentially an attorney.

A classic example of the dangers of well-intended yet inaccurate communication with patients recently occurred in my own practice. An elderly cancer patient admitted to a hospital client of mine was very unexpectedly found dead in his hospital room bathroom in the middle of the night. Very appropriately, the patient's family was immediately informed of this tragic occurrence. Unfortunately, the initial person to make contact with the family was a licensed vocational nurse who, immediately after arriving at the scene, jumped to the conclusion that the patient had fallen and sustained some type of fatal injury. She reported this information to the family as if it were an established fact. The first responding nursing manager, who arrived later on the scene, became concerned about the possibility that the patient, who had a terminal diagnosis and was facing the prospect of a potentially painful end of life decline as the result of his disease process, may have actually attempted to harm himself. That possibility was then suggested to the family hours after they were told that the death was the result of a simple fall. The family was deeply offended by the suggestion that the patient may have attempted to harm himself. Furthermore, the two totally inconsistent explanations given to the family immediately after learning that their loved one had died unexpectedly generated a profound lack of trust, bordering on hostility, towards the hospital. Not surprisingly under the circumstances, the family almost immediately turned to an attorney for help. Litigation against the hospital then ensued.

Only after litigation had been initiated did a more complete and detailed investigation reveal what truly happened to this unfortunate patient. In a bizarre yet unforeseeable accident, a central line catheter used for the patient's cancer treatment had become dislodged, and the patient had suffered a fatal air embolism. By the time the truth was finally understood, however, the litigation process was too far along to be easily aborted. Although the hospital was ultimately exonerated at trial, it took several years of litigation and hundreds of thousands of dollars in expenses to achieve that "successful" result.

Of course, there is no way to say with certainty that litigation would not have resulted over this unusual death, even if the initial communication with the family had been handled in a better fashion. However, it is not illogical to assume that the chances of litigation could have been at least significantly reduced had misleading and ultimately inaccurate information regarding the cause of death not been relayed to the family at their most emotionally vulnerable moment in time. There is no doubt that every member of the hospital staff who communicated with the family that night did so with absolutely the best of intentions, hoping only to be as helpful as they could be to the family at that most difficult time. But while their intentions were admirable and well-motivated, there is also little doubt that the communication actions taken in this case ultimately failed to help anyone involved.

A simple solution exists to this problem: All bedside healthcare practitioners should receive proper training that empowers them to appropriately answer the questions they so often face from patients.

> *"All bedside healthcare practitioners should receive proper training that empowers them to appropriately answer the questions they so often face from patients."*

But at the same time, such bedside professionals should be cautioned against attempting to answer questions that are clearly beyond their professional expertise. Instead, they should be reminded of how important it is to validate those questions and ensure they are answered both timely and accurately.

In-service training sessions on communication are an effective and relatively low-cost method of achieving this goal. An in-house team comprised of both legal and clinical administrative members can conduct these sessions. Teaching bedside staff to follow a simple process to respond to difficult questions in the following four-part manner can effectively diminish, if not eliminate, this problem:

1. Acknowledge the validity and importance of the question.
2. Admit candidly that the question is beyond the person's ability to answer completely.
3. Specifically identify the person or persons who can answer the question.

4. Provide the patient with a specific and realistic time frame for when the question will be referred to that person and an answer provided.

In summary, practitioners cannot effectively manage the healthcare-liability legal risks they face without first truly understanding why certain patients turn into medical-legal adversaries. A fatalistic disrespect of the medical-legal process and the motivations of people who turn to it is neither accurate, justified nor helpful. Practitioners need to understand that even the highest-quality care will not eliminate all medical-legal risk if their patients are not educated about their own health status and the realistic limitations of modern medicine. Even patients who receive superb care can find themselves in the position where they may feel motivated, if not obligated, to seek legal advice to answer their healthcare questions.

In my professional career I have seen a large number of patients and families face the reality of either a less than perfect medical outcome or even the ultimately unavoidable prospect of death and yet remain totally satisfied with the healthcare they or their loved one received. I have also seen patients who have truly made miraculous recoveries because of heroic medical intervention turn to the legal process for redress over a minor issue simply because that minor problem was not properly anticipated, not properly explained or both. Achieving patient satisfaction — as much or more than achieving patient healing — is often the key to preventing patients from turning into medical plaintiffs. Recognizing that fact and acting on it before you begin your care of any individual patient is perhaps the single greatest thing you can do as a practitioner to prospectively manage your professional healthcare-liability legal risk.

CHAPTER 2

Managing Expectations

With few exceptions, every healthcare practitioner I have known has done his or her utmost to provide quality care and to achieve the best possible outcomes for his or her patients. I hope my many colleagues in the healthcare defense bar can make the same statement about their professional practices. It is a simple and widely held belief among the practitioners I have known that providing the highest-quality care in and of itself is the best protection against medical-legal risk. However, this is not an entirely accurate understanding, in my judgment, of how medical risks develop and how they can be prospectively managed. While providing the highest-quality care is necessary for reducing and managing medical-legal risk, it alone is not sufficient.

Many practitioners have provided exemplary care and achieved nearly miraculous results and yet still faced either significant medical liability or medical-legal risk. I believe the single most significant reason behind this unfortunate reality is that even the best practitioners often fail to address and appropriately manage the expectations of their patients and their patients' families.

Managing patient and patient family expectations must start before the treatment or procedure ever begins. It must be based on an open, frank and honest dialogue with a patient and/or his or her family about the nature of a medical procedure, its likely benefits and realistic risks. Too often, however, no such dialogue ever takes place before significant care is provided.

Perhaps this type of conversation is rare because of our inherent discomfort with discussing the issues that simply must be discussed under the circumstances. Most clinicians will recognize and acknowledge that nothing makes many patients more uncomfortable than talking candidly about serious medical risks relating to mortality. This inherent — and to a certain degree understandable — reluctance is often compounded by the practitioner's fear of scaring the patient out of consenting to the recommended course of treatment. This often results in the practitioner discussing the true significant risks of a procedure or treatment only in the barest details.

In every jurisdiction in the United States virtually all significant non-emergent procedures require the informed consent of the patient prior to the procedure. Laws governing informed consent have become so ubiquitous and detailed that in the real world of healthcare delivery the process sometimes becomes nothing more than another part of the automated pre-procedure routine. Preprinted forms document informed consent. The actual task of speaking with the patient about legal informed-consent issues is often delegated to medical residents, nurses or even nonclinical office staff. The net result of this unfortunate but common practice is that while the legal formalities of informed consent are often obtained, a true understanding of the nature of a medical procedure or a significant illness is never achieved by the patient and his or her family.

A dangerous disconnect between the patient's expectations and the realistic achievable medical goals often arises when patients fail to gain this type of clear understanding before the initiation of healthcare treatment. This is especially true when the underlying medical condition and/or the procedure the patient is contemplating involves life-threatening risks. An Iraqi cardiovascular surgeon I have known for years is fond of saying, "Americans are the only people on earth who think that death is optional." Many people who work in the healthcare arena can attest to the accuracy of that statement from personal experience.

Virtually no one wants to seriously contemplate, in advance, the possibility of an adverse healthcare outcome, even when the underlying medical situation makes such an outcome likely if not almost unavoidable. When this natural optimism or belief in our own immortality is coupled with a healthcare practitioner's failure to directly and accurately discuss the realities of a disease process and a healthcare treatment regime, the end result is often confusion at best and anger at worst. Confused, angry patients are much more likely to seek the advice of attorneys irrespective of the outcome of their treatment.

It is important that healthcare practitioners not scare patients from consenting to needed, safe and legitimate medical procedures. However, there is a proper balance between the need to avoid discouraging patients from consenting to necessary medical treatments and the need to ensure that those same patients fully understand the nature of their disease process and the possible complications or negative consequences of the medical treatments they are undertaking. Many healthcare practitioners fail to take the necessary steps to appropriately strike the proper balance here. Because of this failure, they often inadvertently increase their litigation and liability risk, irrespective of the quality of the care they provide to their patients.

Practitioners should remember that, despite the medical miracles they often perform on a daily basis, human mortality remains stubbornly stuck at 100 percent. Every practitioner will encounter all types of complications, large and small, expected and unexpected. For these reasons, they should discuss complications — both large and small, likely and remote — openly and candidly with their patients. In my experience, this almost never dissuades patients from obtaining the medical care they need to treat a serious medical condition. To the contrary, in my experience at least the honesty involved in this type of discussion creates a level of trust and confidence that strengthens the physician–patient relationship.

> *"Along with the true details of the end-of-life process, patients often do not understand the balancing of risks that goes into so many important medical decisions."*

A related issue is that although practitioners regularly face difficult, complex and highly subjective treatment decisions, they often fail to share with patients the thought processes behind these decisions. Along with the true details of the end-of-life process, patients often do not understand the balancing of risks that goes into so many important medical decisions practitioners must often make. It is only when patients understand that one risk may necessarily be accepted or even potentially increased to minimize another one that they have a better and more accurate appreciation of adverse situations when they develop.

To illustrate this point, here is an example from my own professional practice. I once tried a lawsuit involving a man who died in a client hospital following surgery to repair a small bowel obstruction. He was profoundly malnourished prior to the surgery. However, to maintain his quality of life his physicians were anxious to restart his gut effectively and quickly following the surgical procedure. For that reason, they decided to refrain from giving him supplemental IV nutrition, even though it was recognized in advance that this might worsen his malnutrition and potentially contribute to skin breakdown. Unfortunately, skin breakdown did occur, and the patient ultimately died from sepsis relating to decubitus ulcers.

His family, however, was never given the opportunity to understand the balancing of risks associated with his malnutrition and bowel obstruction. All they knew was their loved one was not given supplemental nutrition, became malnourished, and developed ultimately fatal skin breakdowns potentially as a result of the nutrition decision. As a result, litigation between the family, the hospital and the patient's physicians ultimately ensued. No one can say with certainty what would have happened if a frank discussion about the balancing of risks had been performed in this case. However, such a discussion could not have hurt the position of the practitioners from a medical-legal standpoint, especially given how the man's clinical course proceeded.

To effectively manage medical-legal risks, practitioners must always remember that it is not the exceptional medical result that avoids medical-legal complications; it is the satisfactory result that accomplishes this important goal. Satisfactory results that are less than optimal from a medical standpoint often manage medical-legal risk better than exceptional medical results involving unexpected complications. I have seen cases involving expected deaths with dignity that have not resulted in medical-legal complications, even when the care involved, from a retrospective analysis, may have been questionable. By the same token, I have seen truly heroic and miraculous work by practitioners that literally saves a patient's life still result in serious litigation, simply because a minor yet unforeseen, unexplained and unexpected complication occurred.

Practitioners rely on the fact that their patients must trust them to perform difficult and often dangerous procedures. Similarly, practitioners should return some of that trust by believing in the ability of their patients to hear the honest truth about both the human condition and the limitations of medicine. By doing so, I am convinced they will find that both their practices and their patients will benefit significantly.

CHAPTER 3

Apologies

As recently as 20 years ago an apology was probably the last thing anyone would expect to hear from a physician or other healthcare specialist. Nurses, technicians, and other bedside healthcare professionals will most likely concur with this statement. The unwillingness and/or inability of healthcare providers to effectively apologize when human error and/or human failings have a negative impact on a patient's medical care has had a profound and, until very recently, unrecognized impact on medical-legal risk. To this day, I do not think most healthcare professionals truly recognize the power of apology as an effective and appropriate medical-legal risk-management tool.

A professional colleague in Texas, who is one of the most successful and well-respected plaintiff's attorneys in my home state, has an interesting view on apologies in the healthcare context. This legal scholar is fond of saying that if doctors would only apologize to patients when adverse events occur, his healthcare-liability plaintiffs practice would essentially be put out of business. While there is a measure of hyperbole in this statement, that measure is rather small. In many circumstances, no single act can be a greater shield from medical-legal problems than an effectively delivered apology.

Over the past few years a significant number of studies have investigated the effect of apologies on patient behavior in the healthcare-liability context. The majority of these studies support the proposition that, when properly delivered, apologies can and do protect healthcare practitioners from medical-legal risk even in cases where medical-legal liability is often abundantly clear. The publication of these studies, however, has led to an overreaction in favor of apologies, in my opinion. Time and again I meet practitioners who seem to believe that apologies are either panaceas, wonder drugs that will treat all ills with a patient, or "one-size-fits-all" tourniquets that can be applied to any patient situation in the same exact fashion with the same exact result. Neither of these assumptions is correct.

Apologies: What would you say?

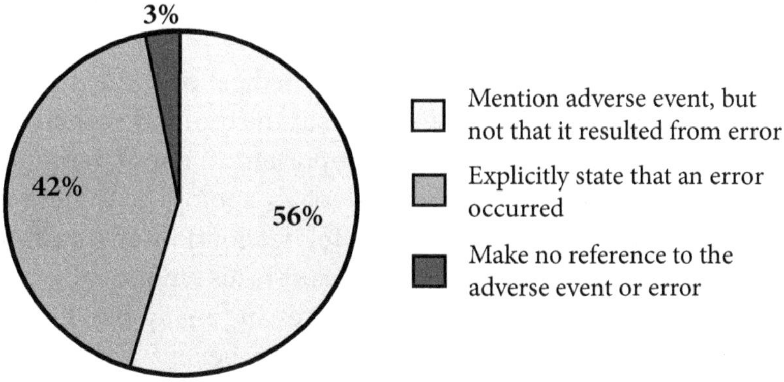

The graph above clearly demonstrates some of the issues the medical community has with apologies following medical complications. Although I certainly cannot prove it, I strongly suspect the tiny 3 percent sliver is in actuality a vast understatement. Making no reference to either an adverse event or an error essentially means making no apology whatsoever. Based on nothing more than over 20 years of professional involvement with medical practitioners, I find it hard to believe that only 3 percent fail to apologize when circumstances warrant it.

Of more interest to me is the very close breakdown between those practitioners who would mention an adverse event but not specifically state it resulted from error and those who would explicitly state that an error occurred. As is outlined in the remaining portion of this chapter, the difference between these two statements lies at the very heart of what constitutes a potentially effective apology and what constitutes something potentially very different and much more dangerous to the speaker. The fact that nearly one in two practitioners who do acknowledge making apologies admit they link the adverse event to a medical error (something I feel is unnecessary and potentially dangerous) indicates to my mind a widespread failure in effective apology management in the healthcare field.

Apologies are essentially no different than any other medicine or medical tool healthcare practitioners potentially use in their daily practice. When used in the appropriate circumstances and with appropriate clinical skill, an apology can be extremely efficacious. However, if used in the wrong circumstances, with the wrong technique, or for the wrong purpose, an apology, like a drug or medical device, can do far more harm than good. Like most things in medicine, the key is how the tool is used.

To properly understand any tool in his medical bag, the clinician must first have an accurate appreciation of what the tool is designed to accomplish. In the case of an apology, it is important to remember that, from a medical-legal standpoint, the purpose of an apology is to redirect negative emotion away from the impulse for retribution or punishment. At its heart, the benefit of an apology is that it heals emotional wounds. It is neither designed for nor capable of addressing many purely intellectual concerns. For that reason, it is often of little benefit if the statement of apology touches on the question of fault for a particular circumstance. It is the expression of sincere and believable regret for the event or outcome that is important. The acceptance of responsibility for that event or outcome often adds little to the emotional healing power of the statement.

From the medical-legal perspective of some clinicians there is little difference between saying "I am sorry you suffered that complication" and saying "I am sorry I caused that complication." However, because the additional acceptance of responsibility adds little to the purpose behind the apology, healthcare practitioners should avoid it when offering apologies in the healthcare context. What should be included, however, is concrete and credible information regarding what the practitioner intends to do going forward to minimize the chances this situation will arise again. Most people who have suffered a medical complication are interested in receiving condolence for that unfortunate occurrence. However, they are often even more interested in knowing, with specificity, what is going to be done to ensure that no other patients find themselves in the same situation. And they are often most interested in hearing that directly from the person offering the apology, contemporaneously with the statement of regret for the injury or the complication at issue. For all of these reasons, in many cases the most effective apology is nothing more than a simple statement containing these two straightforward elements: (1) a sincere, heartfelt and direct expression of regret for the negative event, and (2) a believable and specific plan of action to prevent the event from occurring to someone else.

Acknowledging errors in an apology statement and directly linking them to a medical complication is also often inappropriate for another simpler and more straightforward reason. Medical complications suffered by patients are often just that; complex, complicated events. Whenever complications or problems arise in complex settings, they are very often the result of many different factors. They are rarely the direct result of a single act or single omission. This fact has long been recognized by professionals who investigate another type of complex adverse events: airplane accidents. Those investigators recognize that it is extraordinarily rare for a single erroneous action or omission to actually cause an airplane crash. Instead, the actions of a large number of people (the pilot, the co-pilot, the ground crew, the air traffic controllers) coupled with a wide range of other nonhuman factors (the weather, the mechanical specifications of the plane, the position of the aircraft in flight at the time of the incident) all often contribute to an accident or other less than ideal flight outcome. Some of the human actions may very well be errors, but many of them, in fact, are not. Furthermore, both the number of human and nonhuman factors involved in an air accident, as well as their relative importance, is almost never known with certainty in the days and weeks following the accident itself.

> *"From a medical-legal standpoint, the purpose of an apology is to redirect negative emotion away from the impulse for retribution or punishment."*

Adverse medical outcomes and complications are very similar in these respects. A medical complication rarely happens as the direct result of the actions or omission of a single healthcare provider. Even such extreme scenarios as operating on the wrong body part often occur not as the result of a single individual's negligent failure, but rather as the end result of a number of separate mistakes and/or mistaken assumptions by a number of separate healthcare providers. In the vast majority of cases, a medical complication results from the complex interplay of numerous decisions and actions made by numerous healthcare practitioners. Additionally, like the weather and the mechanical structure of an airplane, the patient's own underlying health condition, including potentially significant comorbidities as well as the circumstances of care (ER, OR, ICU, etc.), all often play important roles. And finally, as is the case with airline accidents, the true interplay of all of these factors is not often apparent until a thorough investigation into the medical incident has occurred.

What this means for the practitioner is that it is often premature at best, and inaccurate at worst, to link a specific perceived error to a medical complication in an apology statement. Keep in mind that to be effective apologies must be made very early in the process of a patient's or patient's family's search for answers and emotional processing of the event which has occurred. In most cases at least, an effective apology must therefore be delivered before a thorough investigation has been made into the medical complication. For this reason as well, explicitly linking a medical complication to an error in an apology statement often involves at least some degree of speculation on the part of the speaker; speculation that can be misleading or in certain cases simply incorrect due to the inherent lack of complete and accurate analysis and information at the time the statement was made.

In short, the key to effective apologies is to say enough to assuage anger and redirect emotional impulse away from the desire for retribution, while at the same time not saying more than is appropriate under the circumstances and thereby creating needless medical-legal risk. Prudent apologies that follow this rule need not be bland and general statements. In fact, they often must be more than that to be credible and therefore useful. Examples of medical apology statements which I believe serve their intended purpose include (but are certainly not limited to):

> "I am deeply sorry for your loss. Your (family member) developed (complication) following the procedure and did not recover. Generally speaking, his medical cause of death was (simple, accurate and understandable explanation). We did (detailed explanation of actions) to minimize the chances of this occurring but could not prevent it. If you have any questions I'd be happy to try and answer them if I can."

> "I am sorry your (family member) did not respond as well as we hoped he would. He developed (complication), which is a (rare/recognized/common) complication of his (procedure/condition/both). (Complication) is generally (simple, accurate and understandable explanation). We did not expect this to occur because (simple, accurate and understandable explanation)," or "We took a number of important steps to minimize the chances of this occurring including (detailed explanation of actions). If you have any questions I'd be happy to try and answer them if I can."

> "I am sorry to report that your (family member) was injured in the facility as the result of (a fall, an accident, etc.) We took a number of specific steps to try and ensure this type of incident would not happen, including (detailed explanation). We will investigate this incident thoroughly both to try and understand how it happened here and improve our (policies, practices) to hopefully ensure this does not happen to any other patient in the future."

By the same token, even seemingly benign yet overly general apology statements can run afoul of the legal risk principles outlined above if care is not given to their exact wording. A few examples of what I feel are less than ideal apology statements include:

> "I am sorry the (surgery/procedure) was unsuccessful (or failed)."

> "I elected to (insert medical choice here) during my care of (patient name). In hindsight I am sorry I made that decision."

If practitioners decide to add the element of fault or responsibility to statements of apology, they open themselves up to potentially significant additional legal risk, above and beyond the legal risk originally caused by the medical complication itself. It is important for all practitioners to remember that apologies, by their very nature, are almost always going to be legally considered exceptions to the hearsay rule. Generally speaking, *hearsay* is the legal term for any out-of-court statement offered at trial to prove the truth of the matter asserted. As a general proposition, hearsay is not admissible evidence in a civil trial in virtually every U.S. jurisdiction. However, there are certain exceptions to the hearsay rule. Put another way, there are certain extenuating circumstances that make an out-of-court statement especially trustworthy — trustworthy enough that the judicial system will allow it in evidence at trial even if it is offered to prove the truth of the matter asserted in the statement itself.

One of these almost universally recognized exceptions is what is known as a *statement against interest*. The fundamental assumption behind this exception is that people will not make statements publicly that are against their personal, financial or other significant interests unless those statements are true. Because of this assumption, statements against interest are judged to be more trustworthy than other out-of-court statements. They are therefore recognized as an exception to the hearsay rule in virtually every jurisdiction in the country.

By their very nature, apologies are inherently statements against interest to one extent or the other. Accordingly, any time you make an apology you should recognize that a jury likely will be allowed to hear that statement if litigation ensues over the event for which you are apologizing. Further, it is important to keep in mind that anyone who overhears the statement against interest will be allowed to repeat it to a jury. This is not limited to the person to whom a practitioner may be apologizing; anyone else within earshot who happened to overhear the statement (or perhaps even part of the statement) could be allowed to repeat it to a jury.

Therefore, it is extremely important to never use words in an apology that you would not want a jury to hear later. Along with admissions of fault, attempts to shift the blame to other healthcare practitioners as part of an apology are also ill-advised for this same reason. Remember that the primary purpose of an apology is to redirect understandable emotional impulses for retribution or punishment in a more positive direction. Merely redirecting those impulses from one target to another does not accomplish this goal. At best, it invites hostility and discord among the healthcare practitioners involved in a particular patient's case. At worst, it can increase the chances of medical-legal complications for everyone by encouraging a patient to become a healthcare-liability plaintiff, something everyone involved in the patient's care should want to avoid.

It is equally important to carefully choose the setting in which an apology is issued. Having a friendly witness present for the delivery of an apology can help ensure that the apology statement is received as it is intended. A second set of friendly ears hearing the exchange and friendly eyes witnessing it can serve as a kind of safety net during the process. Because of the emotionally stressful nature of making an apology of this type, the person offering the apology is often not best positioned to accurately evaluate how it is received. A friendly witness, particularly one who is trained and experienced in the use of apologies as a medical-legal risk-litigation tool, often makes the difference between an apology that is well received and one that is not. While an understanding of the medical-legal implications of an apology is an asset for this friendly witness, a law degree itself often is not. By that I mean that the physical presence of either a practitioner's or an institution's lawyer at the delivery of an apology is often counter-productive, for what are probably obvious reasons. Another healthcare colleague or healthcare administrator with an understanding of both the proper purposes of good apologies and the potential dangers of bad ones is almost always a more ideal friendly witness. The presence of a friendly witness during the delivery of an apology can also prevent what is commonly referred to as a "swearing match" at trial — the situation where the only two witnesses to a statement tell fundamentally different versions of that statement to a jury, leaving them with the unenviable task of deciding who to believe without the benefit of additional evidence.

An even greater danger is that a poorly worded apology may constitute what is known as a legal admission. If the apology includes a specific enough admission of medical fault, and if the person making the apology is sufficiently qualified from a medical standpoint to offer opinions on medical causation, the poorly worded apology could potentially be considered a legal admission of fault. That means the statement could be considered substantial or even conclusive evidence of fault against the person making the statement. For example, an emergency room doctor who makes a statement such as, "I am sorry I took off the cervical collar when I did; I took it off too early, and that caused the fracture to displace," could have that statement be considered substantial or even conclusive proof of both medical liability and causation against that physician at trial.

Even more ominously from a medical-legal perspective, if the apology statement is deemed to be in admission in the truest sense, it is possible that the attorney representing the person who made the poorly worded apology could be precluded from challenging his or her statement at trial. In other words, the person making the legal admission could be precluded at trial from challenging that admission through the introduction of contradictory evidence (i.e., supportive testimony from a defense expert). Certainly, this is a much less likely scenario than the one discussed earlier with the hearsay rule, but it is a real theoretical possibility that should not be ignored.

Finally, poorly worded apologies can have a negative impact long before trial. They can endanger a practitioner's insurance coverage for a medical-legal claim and, in a worst-case scenario, do so significantly and/or irreversibly. Virtually all professional liability insurance policies contain clauses requiring that the insured practitioner cooperate fully in his or her own defense. A poorly worded apology, especially if it contains an unequivocal admission of fault, could easily be viewed as a failure to provide that contractually required cooperation.

Depending on the language of the particular professional liability insurance policy at issue, that failure could potentially justify an insurance company's refusal to continue to provide coverage for a medical-legal claim. This refusal could not only encompass the denial of coverage in the event of an adverse finding of liability and award of damages, but it could also include a refusal to pay ongoing attorneys' fees inherently associated with the defense regardless of the ultimate outcome of the case. This too is a somewhat unlikely occurrence; however, the consequences of this scenario arising can be so grave that they should never be ignored by any practitioner considering an apology to a patient following an adverse medical event.

Apologies are indeed powerful weapons. But like most powerful weapons, they can be used for good or ill. When used properly, an apology can be an extremely valuable tool for preventative legal care. However, like all tools associated with a medical practitioner's trade, great care must be taken to learn about apologies and their proper handling before they are used on real patients with real consequences.

CHAPTER 4

The Medical Record

The patient's medical record, not surprisingly, is the single most important document in determining the medical-legal risk faced by a practitioner in any given situation. Both defense counsel and the plaintiff's counsel utilize the medical record extensively and in a wide variety of ways throughout the course of medical-liability litigation. Everyone knows and fully expects that it will be at the center of the evidence in virtually any medical-liability case. However, what many practitioners fail to recognize is the importance the medical record plays in the preliminary stages of a medical-liability lawsuit and the unique manner in which plaintiff's attorneys use it at that time.

The initial decision to accept or reject a potential claimant is one of the most important decisions a plaintiff's attorney has to make. Quite literally tens of thousands of dollars, and in some cases hundreds of thousands of dollars or more, are at stake every time a plaintiff's attorney evaluates a patient who is seeking representation in a lawsuit against a healthcare provider. The plaintiff's attorney is likely fronting 100 percent of the costs of the suit, so making the wrong decision and accepting patients with meritless claims is a quick road to bankruptcy and the end of the attorney's professional practice. Similarly, if the plaintiff's attorney misevaluates a case and turns down a claim with significant merit (and significant damages), he or she almost certainly hands a potential financial windfall to a competitor, perhaps leading to a lifetime's worth of second guessing if that competitor turns the case into a significant financial reward for both attorney and client.

Many practitioners fail to fully appreciate the pivotal role the medical record plays when a plaintiff's attorney is making this critical initial decision. The medical record is so important at this early stage because of the limited sources of information that are available to a plaintiff's lawyer when evaluating a case at its onset. Of course, at that moment in time the attorney has the full benefit of the potential client's version of the facts. However, not surprisingly, few potential clients of a medical malpractice plaintiff's attorney are themselves healthcare practitioners. Their version of the facts, therefore, almost always lacks the type of educated foundation that is essential for medical accuracy. Furthermore, the significant emotion that always accompanies serious adverse healthcare events often colors the patient's version of what happened or the version told by the patient's family. For both of these reasons, as most plaintiff's attorneys will admit, they must take the version of the medical facts told by a potential claimant/client with at least a grain of salt.

I doubt you will find many plaintiff's attorneys who would not wish for better opportunities to thoroughly investigate the patient's or family's story before deciding whether to accept a case and file a lawsuit. Oddly enough, in the name of tort reform many states have significantly restricted the ability of plaintiff's attorneys to conduct this type of investigation, thereby significantly increasing the difficulty plaintiff's attorneys have in differentiating between meritorious and unmeritorious claims. A major part of many states' tort-reform legislation over the past ten to fifteen years has been prohibitions against presuit and/or early litigation discovery in medical-liability cases. The rationale behind these tort-reform changes is a desire to spare practitioners (or perhaps more accurately, their insurance carriers) the cost associated with involving defense counsel in the presuit or preliminary discovery process. However, the real-world result of these provisions is to take away a generally useful and usually minimally invasive tool used by competent and careful plaintiff's attorneys to evaluate a case before filing it.

Thus, when making the critical decision to accept or reject a patient's case, in many jurisdictions a plaintiff's attorney is often left with only one neutral and reliable source of information: the medical record. In many cases the decision to accept or reject a client has to be made almost exclusively based on what is and is not documented in that medical chart. Given the weight of that initial decision, the importance of the medical chart as an instrument of medical-legal risk truly cannot be overstated.

Another important yet little known and understood fact is the way in which a plaintiff's attorney uses the medical chart during this critical initial decision-making process. It is no exaggeration to say that during this process the chart is used in a manner for which it was never intended. This is not the result of any type of intentional misuse of the chart by the plaintiff's attorney. It is merely an unavoidable result of the way our legal system forces medical-liability cases to be evaluated at this critical stage.

First, the chart is not used in any type of contemporaneous fashion. Fundamentally, the primary function of the medical chart is to provide information contemporaneously with the treatment that it documents. This is especially true for an acute-care hospital chart, which is the type of medical record a professional liability plaintiff's attorney most often evaluates. However, in most cases, at a bare minimum it is weeks if not months after a medical event has occurred before a family member considers contacting a plaintiff's attorney to pursue a medical-legal claim. Even in the unusual case in which a patient comes to an attorney within weeks of the medical event at issue, it can be additional weeks after that before the medical chart is provided to the plaintiff's attorney for review. In many cases, months and sometimes entire years elapse between the time of the medical event in question and the patient's initial consultation with a plaintiff's attorney. Contemporaneous evaluation of the medical chart with the patient is therefore virtually impossible for a plaintiff's attorney utilizing a medical record.

"When making the critical decision to accept or reject a patient's case, in many jurisdictions a plaintiff's attorney is often left with only one neutral and reliable source of information: the medical record."

Second, the plaintiff's attorney in a very real sense is forced to utilize the medical chart essentially in a vacuum, which usually never occurs when practitioners use the chart in a clinical setting. The vacuum exists because a plaintiff's attorney who uses a medical record to evaluate a case does so without the benefit of two additional sources of information that clinicians utilizing a chart would always have at their disposal. The first of these is the clinical team attending any given patient. Any time a clinician cannot find information in the medical chart, he or she can always ask for that information from one of his or her colleagues. The second and even more valuable source of information supplementing the chart is the patient himself. Even in cases in which the patient is nonresponsive, he or she is often an extremely valuable source of information, through medical-monitoring equipment if nothing else.

The lack of these two contemporaneous sources of information with which to supplement the medical chart can lead to a number of dubious, if not outright erroneous, conclusions about care in the medical-legal evaluation process. The first of these will be familiar to most readers of this book: the concept that if something is "not documented, it is not done." This statement is used as a teaching tool at medical education institutions around the country, and there are probably few statements that irritate medical-legal defense counsel more than this one. The most fundamental reason for this, in my opinion, is that the statement itself is simply not true in any real respect. If one analyzes the situation objectively, it becomes clear that there are three possibilities for a particular medical task with a particular patient.

A: The task can be done and documented;

B: The task can be done but not documented; or

C: The task can be documented but not done.

In the abstract, no one of the three options above is, theoretically, any more likely than the other one. However, more often than not in the real world legal specialists evaluating a medical record jump to the conclusion of "not documented, not done." This can lead plaintiff's attorneys to reach the preliminary conclusion that negligent care was provided merely because of negligent documentation.

Certainly no plaintiff's attorney wishes to draw the wrong conclusion on this critical question at this critical time. However, in my experience it is a simple fact that this assumption, based on this use of the chart, does indeed occur and with relative frequency. Although subsequent discovery often reveals circumstances in which the "not documented, not done" fallacy has erroneously led to an initial conclusion that negligent care was provided, that is usually no solace to the practitioner involved in the lawsuit. By the time the truth is revealed, the practitioner has experienced significant stress, time loss, distraction, and sometimes personal expense by virtue of being forced to engage in pretrial discovery and adversarial litigation. In a real sense the practitioner has still lost, even if he or she may prevail ultimately on the merits of the claim, simply because the claim has been filed. To the extent the claim was filed because of poor documentation, it is a medical-legal risk that preventative legal care could have potentially avoided.

The second logical fallacy that can result from this unorthodox but necessary use of the medical chart by plaintiff's attorneys is a corollary to "not documented, not done": "not documented, not known." Put simply, this is the often erroneous conclusion that if a piece of information is not expressly documented in the medical record, the practitioners caring for a patient did not know it or consider it when making potentially critical healthcare decisions. For example, if a particular set of vital signs is not documented prior to a surgical procedure, one can draw the conclusion that the surgeon and/or anesthesiologist did not know those vital signs before making decisions. If surgical complications occurred, they could be erroneously attributed to the lack of that information, thereby implying medical fault on the part of the surgeon, the anesthesiologist, the nursing staff or all of the above.

"All the medical chart is intended to be is a good-faith effort to accurately document information that appeared relevant and important to the patient's care and/or useful to other practitioners involved with the patient at the time it was obtained."

In the real world, when information is not documented in the medical chart it is almost always available from one of the two aforementioned contemporaneous sources: the clinical-care team or the patient. In fact, as a practical matter, those two sources of information are often equally or more important than the medical chart in conveying the type of critical decision-making information that is truly needed for proper medical decisions to be made. The idea that the medical chart is supposed to be like a courtroom transcript, capturing every syllable of every statement made about a patient during the entire course of a hospitalization, is simply not accurate. All the medical chart is intended to be is a good-faith effort to accurately document information that appeared relevant and important to the patient's care and/or useful to other practitioners involved with the patient at the time it was obtained. Nothing more is truly intended from the medical chart, despite the fact that we in the legal profession often expect much more from it.

The critical fact here is that the members of the legal profession often expect much more from the medical chart than is intended by many clinical providers who contribute to it. The potential medical-legal dangers associated with the "not documented, not known" assumption are virtually identical to those discussed earlier with respect to the "not documented, not done" adage. If a plaintiff's attorney concludes that substandard care was provided based on an erroneous "not documented, not known" conclusion, it will be little solace to a practitioner if he or she is able to correct that fallacy only after the onset of litigation. Preventing the potentially dangerous assumption from the outset through knowledgeable and careful charting is the only truly satisfactory approach from a medical-legal risk-management prospective.

Because the medical chart plays such a pivotal role in a plaintiff's attorneys decision on whether or not to accept a case, a prudent medical practitioner will take great care when deciding how to document in it. Preventative legal care demands that every medical practitioner recognize that their charting will be read not only by their peers and colleagues but also, at one time or another, by their medical-legal adversaries. Every entry in the chart should always be made with that thought in mind. This is not to say that charting should ever be done in a way that does not advance the medical needs of the patient. It is merely to say that the entirely compatible, mutually applicable goal of preventive legal care should also be followed when charting a patient at all times.

Further, practitioners who design charting systems should also heed all of these same lessons. To do otherwise is to place practitioners squarely in the crosshairs of unnecessary medical-legal risk through poorly designed documentation systems. For example, needless and often mindless checklists in medical charts are often nothing more than a recipe for failure. Requiring that a particular staff member chart on a particular page in a particular checkbox at a particular time almost guarantees that charting omissions will occur over the course of a long hospitalization. When those charting omissions do occur, they often lead to the type of conclusions described above and to lawsuits being filed when ultimately neither the practitioner nor the plaintiff's attorney honestly wishes they were pursued.

In conclusion, preventative legal care requires effective management of documentation risks because your legal adversaries start with your documentation when evaluating claims against you. Understanding how, when, and why a plaintiff's attorney utilizes the medical chart is the first step toward minimizing the legal risks that erroneous, ill-advised or inappropriate charting can create. A plaintiff's attorney takes great time and great care in analyzing a medical chart to identify potential medical liability. A wise practitioner will spend at least as much time and commit at least as much care to analyzing his or her own medical charting in an effort to minimize the unnecessary creation of medical-legal risk.

CHAPTER 5

Policies and Procedures

One often overlooked area of manageable but often mismanaged medical-legal risk lies with institutional policies and procedures. In many cases either accrediting institutions, state governing boards or a combination of the two mandate the existence of these procedures. And in many cases the substantive content of clinical policies and procedures is of great benefit to patients. Even something as simple as the standardization of important healthcare procedures in written policies has undeniably improved the quality and consistency of care provided to patients in many circumstances. However, written clinical policies and procedures also have a potential dark side. They often represent a significant and generally overlooked medical-legal danger to both the institutions that adopt them and the practitioners who follow them.

This danger is often unappreciated in part because many clinicians do not recognize the legal importance of their clinical medical policies. For this reason, the problems with policies from a medical-legal standpoint almost always start with their inception. I have seen many situations in which clinical institutions create written clinical policies with no legal review or oversight. Clinical managers or even low-level clinical practitioners may simply write policies as they see fit. Other clinical staff members then review or revise those policies on a regular or semi-regular basis. However, a healthcare facility's legal counsel rarely sees those policies until they become important in pending litigation. By that point it is far too late to appropriately and prospectively manage the legal risks these policies can create.

It is a little known fact that plaintiff's medical-malpractice attorneys often create shared libraries of clinical policies and procedures from healthcare institutions. These documents are often requested en masse during litigation and are often produced en masse by defense counsel who do not always adequately appreciate the longer-term danger to their clients that this type of voluntary and unnecessary overproduction of written policies can present. The creation of policy libraries by plaintiff's attorneys provides those attorneys with a window into the clinical thinking of an institution before a lawsuit is even filed. It also allows those same attorneys to recognize when institutional changes in the instructions for clinical care have been delivered. Both of these benefits give plaintiff's attorneys substantial advantages when evaluating whether to take a particular case and against which healthcare institutions to file it, when such choices exist.

However, the more important problem with policies and procedures lies in their authors' single-minded focus on the policies' clinical impact to the exclusion of any consideration of the policies' medical-legal effect. This leads to situations in which clinical policies are worded in ways that unnecessarily create legal risks — i.e., situations in which a policy creates a legal risk unrelated to the clinical benefit it delivers to patients. Hospital policies and procedures should always be written in the manner best suited to the delivery of high-quality care, irrespective of their legal consequences. Nothing in this chapter is intended to contradict that statement. The medical-legal problem with written policies and procedures arises when a policy is drafted in such a way that it creates a legal risk wholly unrelated to the clinical benefit the policy provides to patients. The most common way this occurs is through ill-advised wording as a result of poor clinical drafting, which is often the result of the drafting of policies by clinical personnel who do not have the necessary and sufficient legal training to recognize the legal implications of the words they choose.

It is absolutely critical that all healthcare providers keep in mind that, like the verbal statements they make to patients, institutional policies are the words of the healthcare defendant. You as the healthcare provider voluntarily chose those words that are the building blocks of your institution's policies and procedures. No one forced you to use the words you selected. When reviewing your policies a jury will recognize these facts without having to be reminded of them, and a good plaintiff's attorney will always repeatedly remind a jury of these facts anyway. A jury therefore will hold both you, the clinical practitioner, as well as the individual or institutional author of a particular policy or procedure, to the plain language of that policy or procedure. A jury will not be receptive to arguments that, in reality, a policy or procedure does not mean what it appears to say on paper.

From a practical standpoint this means that juries will almost always ascribe common-sense definitions to terms used in medical policies even if the author of the policy had a different meaning in mind when it was written. An example from my own practice comes to mind. A hospital client of mine once had a written policy requiring that fall prevention protocols be put in place for "all" patients over a certain age. In practice, however, the hospital's actual policy was to put those protocols in place only if a patient's clinical presentation, above and beyond simple age, justified them in some way. Not surprisingly, during a trial involving an undeniably vigorous and mobile yet elderly patient (age above the threshold set in the protocol) who fell in the absence of fall prevention measures, the jury was less than impressed by the hospital's interpretation of its own written policy. To the jury, the use of the term "all" in the policy meant just what it said, irrespective of the meaning the hospital wanted to ascribe to that simple term.

Another problem can arise when healthcare practitioners inadvertently use terms with legal meaning in the wording of clinical healthcare policies. Because a jury evaluating clinical healthcare policies always does so in a legal setting, the jury members can be predisposed to apply the strict legal meaning to a legal term of art used in a medical policy, irrespective of whether that was the policy author's intention. And once again, good plaintiffs' attorneys can always be counted on to encourage juries to apply legal definitions to legal terms in medical documents, especially when that interpretation will help their clients at trial.

The most egregious example of this second type of wording problem is a policy that attempts to label or define the clinical standard of care. "Standard of care" is a legal term of art in virtually every jurisdiction. It is almost always the ultimate factual question to be decided by a jury. "Negligence" in the medical-legal sense is the failure to follow the standard of care when caring for a patient. Thus, in and of itself, the failure to follow the standard of care is in theory sufficient to entitle a plaintiff to a monetary award against a defendant healthcare provider, provided that the failure to follow the standard of care in question was a cause of the patient's ultimate injury or complication.

In most if not all jurisdictions, the "standard of care" in a medical situation is what is known as ordinary care — that is, doing what an ordinary clinician of reasonable prudence would do under the same or similar circumstances. Although this often surprises medical practitioners, the legal term of art "standard of care" is almost never defined by statute with any more specificity than that. This allows healthcare providers a wide degree of latitude in explaining how their care of a particular patient met the standard of care during the course of a medical-liability lawsuit. That latitude is often critical to the successful defense of any medical-malpractice claim.

However, if an institution unilaterally and voluntarily decides to write a policy that it terms as the "standard of care," all bets are off. The exact words of that written policy, the plaintiff's attorney will argue, now constitutes the voluntary adopted, binding legal standard of care applicable to the institution in question for the patient care at issue. Even the slightest derivation from the exact wording of the policy will be argued to be a violation of the standard of care, sufficient in and of itself to mandate a verdict for the plaintiff if it can be causally linked to the injury at issue. In the face of such a policy, a defendant will find it difficult, if not impossible, to make a jury understand how the care provided to a patient was fundamentally reasonable and appropriate. The question will simply be whether or not every single detail of the policy labeled "standard of care" was strictly and completely followed. Since policies are often varied from, to one degree or another, due to completely appropriate and reasonable individual differences in patients and in practices, this can lead to severe problems defending even the best care at trial.

> *"Negligence in the medical-legal sense is the failure to follow the standard of care when caring for a patient."*

Only slightly less problematic than the labeling of a policy as a "standard of care" is the labeling of a policy as a "rule" or "regulation." In the minds of most laymen without medical training, rules and regulations are far different from policies. Rules and regulations must be followed. They cannot be varied from with appropriate discretion. They can only be violated or broken.

Policies, on the other hand, are more appropriately thought of as guidelines. They can be followed, or alternatively, under the right circumstances, they can be varied from when it is in the best interest of the patient to do so. However, the ability to explain this critical difference hinges almost entirely on the word usage in the policy. If a policy is appropriately labeled as a guideline, this argument will often make sense and be persuasive. If a policy is labeled as a rule or regulation, however, the situation is reversed. A jury is much less likely to believe that any variance from the strict interpretation of the written words in the document is appropriate, regardless of the clinical facts of a particular case.

All of these problems with policies are compounded when they include what I call "absolute" words. These are, generally speaking, words that on their face limit or eliminate the discretion of the healthcare provider providing care in accordance with the policy. The most obvious and critical of these are words such as "must," "always," "never," and "shall." An equally important but less obvious absolute word is "immediately." Again, it is critical that healthcare providers keep in mind that laymen attribute ordinary meanings to these ordinary words. "Must" means without any exception. "Immediately" means just that, without any delay irrespective of circumstances. "Never" means under no circumstances whatsoever.

The following is an example from my own professional experience. During a project to review institutional clinical care policies for a long term care facility client, I came across the following language in a wound care assessment policy:

> "The Registered Nurse shall document the required information on wound status using the Wound Assessment Form every 24 hours."

In this particular institution, the Wound Assessment Form was a separate document, which was not always part of a patient's initial chart. It therefore had to be located among separate paper supplies before it could be used in any given patient's case. (Obviously this example predates the widespread introduction of electronic medical records; however, it is instructive nonetheless.) As you might expect, sometimes nurses in the midst of a busy day would not find the time to go get the additional form and add it to a patient's chart immediately upon recognition of a wound. Additionally, and again understandably, occasions sometimes arose when a nurse could not find a copy of this particular form when it was needed to supplement a particular patient's chart. When either scenario unfolded, the nurses involved typically documented all the required information; however, they did so using a different method and an alternative location in the existing medical chart.

No one would argue with the benefits to patient care from having an institutional policy designed to ensure that accurate and timely information regarding patient wounds is appropriately documented in the patient's medical record. That being said, consider for a moment all of the strict mandates contained in this policy segment as written. Mandates which, at least arguably, contribute little or nothing to the quality of patient care achieved by the policy itself. For example, why is it necessary to require that the documentation be done by the registered nurse? Note the use of the absolute word "shall" in that section of the policy. Further note that the policy does not mandate that the wound assessment itself be performed by the RN (which could perhaps have clinical benefit to the patient); only that the documentation be done exclusively by the registered nursing provider. Why couldn't a busy RN be allowed to do the wound assessment and delegate the documentation task to a subordinate, particularly if there were no changes in the patient's condition? What detriment would there be to patient care if this purely documentation discretion was recognized in the policy itself?

Additionally, why must a particular additional form be used for documenting this information? Once again, why shouldn't a nurse be permitted to document this information in her nursing narrative or some other easily accessible place in the medical chart? Finally, why mandate a documented assessment every 24 hours? If 25 hours passed between assessments, is that necessarily inappropriate? Does it necessarily constitute substandard care of the patient?

Based on input from the facility's in-house counsel and our office, this particular policy provision was amended to read as follows:

> "The registered nurse shall complete an assessment of the patient's wound every 24 hours or as the patient's condition warrants. That assessment shall be timely documented either on the Wound Assessment Form or in another appropriate portion of the patient's medical record."

In its original form, this policy language was a classic example of what I call "policies doomed to fail." By that I mean policies with a combination of rigid and unnecessary requirements unrelated to the quality of care; requirements that ultimately will be violated by the fallible humans tasked with compliance. Put another way, it is only a matter of time before some nurse, probably with the very best of intentions, violates this policy as originally written in some fashion. However, that inevitable violation of the policy as originally worded could easily make no difference whatsoever in the care of the patient. Yet purely because of the original wording of the policy, the same violation, which was likely clinically insignificant to the patient, could be a key point of contention in any medical-legal battle that may subsequently arise over patient care.

In many if not most healthcare institutions, clinical polices are often only reviewed every few years. Therefore it is not hard to imagine how clinical circumstances can arise that would arguably justify, if not professionally mandate, some degree of flexibility from the exact wording of the procedures outlined in any given clinical policy. However, if the policy in question is labeled the standard of care, a rule, or regulation, or if the policy in question contains absolute words such as those listed above, even medically justifiable variations can seem to be negligent care. Certainly, a thoughtful and skilled plaintiff's attorney will argue that the variation constituted negligent care. Thus, at a minimum, a healthcare practitioner defendant who authors and implements these types of policies will be faced with the unenviable task of countering that argument in addition to crafting the necessary medical arguments to defend the care at issue in a medical-malpractice lawsuit. Often this additional burden of defense is sufficient in and of itself to turn even a factually dubious medical lawsuit into one with sufficient risk of an adverse finding of liability to justify monetary settlement.

A much better approach toward preventative medical care with respect to policies and procedures is to include a legal review of all policies, both when they are written and when they are revised. Certainly, the legal reviewer should not interfere with the clinical purposes of the policy itself. Rather, he or she should simply join the drafting and revision process to ensure that the clinical goals of the policy are met without unnecessarily endangering either the institution adopting the policy or the practitioner following it as a result of simple but legally significant wording errors. When done properly, the involvement of legal personnel in the policy-drafting process should not in any way diminish the clinical benefit rendered by the policy. It merely provides an effective and cost-efficient method of managing the medical-legal risk associated with policies and procedures in the best spirit of preventative legal care.

CHAPTER 6

Technology and Legal Risk

Throughout the history of medicine, the advancement of technology has done more to change the nature and practice of healthcare than probably any other single factor. However, with all of the improvements and advances technology has brought for patients, it has also brought accompanying new medical-legal risks for practitioners. This is a classic example of the timeless adage that risk and reward are two sides of the same coin; one rarely exists without the other.

In terms of medical-legal risk, no single technological innovation has probably been more important over the past decade than the invention and widespread use of electronic medical records (EMRs). EMRs promise a wide variety of benefits to patients, including improved access to a patient's full medical history, faster notification of test results, treatments and consultations, availability of more comprehensive patient history information to practitioners, and last but not least, guaranteed legibility of medical records. The magnitude of these benefits is undeniably substantial. Some studies indicate that as many as 2.2 million adverse notification events and 400,000 deaths could be avoided through a 90 percent adoption of EMRs system wide in all 50 states. Proponents of national EMR adoption also estimate that the total savings from only a 90 percent EMR nationwide adoption rate could exceed $80 billion annually after 15 years.

The medical-legal risks associated with EMR systems start with the fundamental fact that the electronic records are inherently different from paper ones in important respects. First, electronic record systems allow for the retention of exponentially greater volumes of medical records than would ever be possible with paper systems. For example, a standard unit of storage in electronic data systems is a terabyte. One terabyte of paper medical records would include more than 100 million individual paper pages, which would be taller than over 50 Empire State Buildings stacked on top of each other.

Second, EMR systems create records that are meaningless if separated from the computer application that created them. A piece of paper remains a piece of paper regardless of where you store it and under what type of light you read it. However, an electronic record, once separated from the computer program through which it was created, can become nothing more than a meaningless set of binary numbers and computer code.

Third, while paper records are static, EMRs by their very nature are dynamic. Unlike paper records, EMRs can be changed in complex and often difficult to discover ways. Many of these changes can be unintentional and/or unappreciated at the time they are made. For example, the simple act of accessing an EMR can, under certain circumstances, change it in fundamental ways. Many types of fundamental changes to an EMR can be all but invisible to the average user of an EMR system, regardless of his or her level of medical sophistication. However, they can be uncovered with forensic computer training and forensic computer technology.

Finally, EMRs contain inherent metadata, which is generally defined as information describing the history, tracking, or management of an electronic document that is embedded in the document itself but is not visible to the routine observer using the document in a routine fashion. Typically, metadata can be "mined" only by computer specialists conducting forensic examinations of the document in question. However, simply because it is not visible does not mean that it is not there.

When properly and accurately mined, metadata can potentially reveal many important things about patient care that would not be demonstrable from a simple paper record. For example, the specific time that progress notes or assessments are actually entered into the record (which in unfortunate circumstances may be different from the date and time written in the text) is often ascertainable through EMR metadata. The amount of time a radiologist spent actually viewing a particular film or study before writing his or her report can conceivably be established through metadata as well. Even something as basic as the amount of time a physician spent with a patient during a visit can potentially be gleaned from metadata relating to the length of time that patient's EMR was called up on the physician's computer screen.

One touted benefit of EMR systems is that they improve the accuracy of medical-record creation. However, studies have shown that this is not necessarily correct. In fact, certain features on EMR systems can allow, and perhaps even encourage, shortcuts that can actually decrease the accuracy of the records created. For example, many EMR systems have "cut and paste" functionality. When used properly, this capability can significantly reduce the time practitioners have to spend creating medical records, thereby leaving more time for direct patient care. However, when used inappropriately, the same technology can result in dangerous clinical plagiarism. One example of this is when practitioners copy older assessments or notes they have previously made in an electronic chart and paste them into later assessments. An even more dangerous example is the scenario in which one practitioner copies the assessment, note or observation of an entirely different person and pastes that prior documentation into his or her new entry in the medical record, as if the observation made and the words chosen were the EMR user's, not someone else's. This type of clinical plagiarism can not only lead to significant patient-care errors but also increase both the density of records as well as their lack of clarity.

Further, EMR systems by their very nature contain new risks that are completely unrelated to their paper-record-keeping ancestors. One of these is the risk of juxtaposition errors, which is inherent in the use of long lists of procedures, laboratory tests, and other items in the EMR systems. Searching for the proper test or procedure in these long, often multiscreen lists can lead to mistakes. This is especially true when the categorization of the list is poorly considered and/or when the practitioner is attempting to split his or her concentration between his or her patient and a computer screen.

Additionally, there is little standardization in EMR functionality across the myriad of manufacturers. No two systems work exactly alike. In today's medical environment, most practitioners will chart on patients in a variety of settings, from various in-patient facilities to professional offices to the home health setting. As more of these institutions adopt EMR systems, practitioners will find themselves having to be familiar with more and different types of EMR functionality during their everyday practice. The more separate and different types of EMR systems a single practitioner has to deal with on a daily basis, the more likely that practitioner will make a simple functionality mistake that may result in a medical record error.

Even something as simple as the move from reading records on paper to reading records on a computer screen creates additional medical-legal risk for the practitioner. Amazingly, in many cases the view of a record from the computer screen does not match the view on paper that practitioners have grown accustom to seeing. Important items in traditional medical-record documents that are routinely contained on a single sheet of paper often take multiple computer screens to view electronically. This problem can be exacerbated by poorly designed EMR systems that provide little or no capability for the practitioner to move back and forth between screens without losing partially entered and completed data.

Even widely touted benefits to EMR systems bring generally unknown additional risks. A classic example of this is the type of automated alerts most EMR systems have for medication errors and other potentially dangerous documentation events. In a very real sense these alarms have become the "car alarms" of the healthcare world. They go off so often, and for so many different reasons, with certain EMR systems that, whether they are willing to admit it or not, many practitioners develop the unfortunate habit of simply ignoring them. In fact, I think it is unfortunate accurate to say that some unwise practitioners often pay no more attention to any of the automated alerts coming from their EMR systems than they do to car alarms going off in the office parking lot. Aside from the most important danger it creates to patient care, the accompanying medical-legal problem with this situation is that the metadata in the EMR system often documents not only the fact that the alarm went off but also the identity of the person who was using the EMR system at that time and who intentionally or unintentionally ignored the alarm.

"It is vitally important that practitioners understand not only the patient-centered benefits provided by their EMR systems but also the practitioner-centered risks associated with those systems."

In summary, it is vitally important that practitioners understand not only the patient-centered benefits provided by their EMR systems but also the practitioner-centered risks associated with those systems. Practitioners who blindly adopt EMR systems will find themselves exposed to all the risks these systems created. Their patients, however, are not likely to benefit from the improvements these same systems can provide. Instead, such practitioners will likely find themselves doing nothing more than creating extraordinarily high volumes (far higher than they could ever dream of creating with paper-based systems) of inaccurate, unhelpful or otherwise of poor quality records. By doing so, those practitioners ironically enough will have increased their medical-legal risk by and through the use of a tool specifically designed to decrease it. The wise practitioner will avoid this unfortunate scenario by practicing preventative legal care and putting in the time and effort necessary to fully understand the pros and cons, advantages and disadvantages of his or her EMR systems sooner rather than later.

CHAPTER 7

Photography

Whenever I speak to a group of clinical practitioners on a medical-legal topic of interest, I invariably get at least one question about the medical-legal implications of clinical photography, regardless of the topic of my actual presentation. The fact that the topic of photography seems to always come up tells me that interest in and perhaps concerns about photography from a medical-legal standpoint are widespread in the clinical community.

More so than most topics, the issue of photography seems to draw strident and hard-line positions among the clinical practitioners with whom I have spoken. Time and again I hear things such as "never photograph unless it is absolutely necessary," "photographs will always hurt you in a lawsuit," or similar knee-jerk reactions. Photography does indeed create its own set of medical-legal risks for practitioners who engage in it; however, it does not lend itself to simple bright line rules of preventative legal care. Like policies and procedures, apologies, and other topics discussed herein, photography can be an important and valuable tool not only for your patients but also for prospectively managing your medical-legal risk. However, like those other tools, the efficacy of photography from a medical-legal standpoint depends to a great extent on the manner in which it is used.

Medical-legal issues relating to photography start before the photograph is taken. Specifically, they start with the legal concept of consent. Consent to photograph is, generally speaking, a topic governed by the state law of the jurisdiction in which the practitioner resides. Those state laws can vary greatly. So the first step for any practitioner when managing legal risks associated with photography is to understand and recognize the consent requirements provided by their state's law.

Further, it is important to remember that consent to photograph is a related but unique and different concept from permission to use or disclose a photograph. Consent to take the photograph itself must be obtained before the question of the photograph's proper use is even considered.

The Joint Commission recommends that "informed consent" be obtained before any photographs are taken of patients in a clinical setting. While the Joint Commission does not define the term "informed consent" in its recommendations, the term is a legal term with a generally accepted definition. Generally speaking, a patient gives his or her "informed consent" only after he or she has been apprised of all of the risks, circumstances, and other factors a reasonable patient would want to know before making a decision. Note that the standard of disclosure is not the risks, circumstances, and factors that a reasonable practitioner would choose to disclose. The standard is expressed in terms of what the lay person receiving the treatment (or in this case the photograph), not the professional providing the care (or in this case taking the photograph), would want to know.

In my experience, consent for photography is often handled in the same ministerial way that consent for clinical procedures is handled in many facilities. Unfortunately, this often consists of nothing more than a low-level employee presenting a form titled "informed consent for photography" with small-print legalese for the patient to sign prior to admission. The signing of this form often creates a rebuttable presumption that proper consent was obtained. However, limiting the process of obtaining informed consent to nothing more than the uninformed signing of what may be an incomprehensible legal form does little if anything to prospectively manage the legal risks associated with photographic consent. As is the case with obtaining informed consent for medical procedures, taking the time to have an actual conversation with your patient about your intent to photograph him or her, as well as the important ancillary issues of how the photograph will be used, who it will be shared with, and how and where it will be stored, is a much more effective preventative legal approach to this issue. Once it is made a routine part of an approach to patients, I believe practitioners will also find that it is neither an onerous nor a time-consuming burden.

Once the hurdle of photographic consent has been cleared, the next medical-legal issues associated with photography concern their use and storage. Federal law, specifically the Health Insurance Portability and Accountability Act (HIPAA), governs both of these questions. The HIPAA privacy rule establishes the national standard for when and how photographs of patients containing "protected health information" (PHI) can be used and disclosed. The HIPAA security rule provides the national standard for how photographs containing protected health information must be stored and safeguarded to ensure against improper use or disclosure. It is important to note that both the HIPAA privacy rule and the HIPAA security rule create legal floors on these topics; they do not create legal ceilings. This means that any individual state has the right to enact more stringent privacy and/or security requirements than what the HIPAA statute contains. However, no state can allow practitioners to take, store, or use photographs covered by HIPAA under weaker privacy or security protections than afforded by federal law.

The only photographs that are covered by either the HIPAA privacy or the HIPAA security rule are those that contain "protected health information." Protected health information is any information that could reasonably be used to identify the patient in question. It is important to note that the information does not have to definitively identify the patient to be PHI. It merely must be something that could reasonably be used to potentially identify the patient. Obvious examples of PHI include names, addresses, and medical record numbers. Less obvious pieces of PHI include dates of birth, dates of service, initials, Social Security numbers, email addresses and even vehicle license plate numbers. This list is not exhaustive, and practitioners would be wise to consult the HIPAA statute itself for a more complete listing if they are concerned about the status of a particular piece of information as potential PHI in a photograph.

"The only photographs that are covered by either the HIPAA privacy or the HIPAA security rule are those that contain 'protected health information.'"

If a photograph contains PHI, generally speaking, it may be used only for treatment, reimbursement, and health administrative management purposes without the express authorization of the patient. There are exceptions to this rule that can apply in certain specific circumstances.

For example, law-enforcement purposes (i.e., the request for a photograph by a sheriff or district attorney), judicial orders, and certain national priority purposes are statutorily recognized exceptions to the HIPAA privacy rule. However, in most circumstances the three general categories of use outlined above (treatment, reimbursement and health administrative management) are the only three a practitioner should feel comfortable engaging in with a photograph containing PHI absent express and informed authorization from the patient for some other type of use.

The HIPAA security rule demands that three types of safeguards be in place for the storage of all materials, including photographs, that contain PHI. The first is administrative safeguards. Generally, administrative safeguards focus on internal organization, policies, procedures, and maintenance of security measures to protect PHI at an institution, Examples of administrative safeguards include but are not limited to: 1) security management processes (designed to identify and analyze potential risks to PHI and implement appropriate measures to reduce them); 2) security personnel (designed to specifically designate employees responsible for developing and implementing PHI security procedures); 3) workforce training and management (designed to provide appropriate authorization and supervision of workforce members who deal with PHI); and 4) evaluations (designed to periodically assess how well other safeguards work in maintaining HIPAA compliance.

The second category is physical safeguards. Generally, physical safeguards are items that govern your practice's ability to protect PHI in its possession from physical threats. Examples of physical safeguards include but are not limited to: 1) facility access and control (designed to limit physical access to a healthcare institution's facilities to ensure unauthorized use of PHI does not occur), and 2) workstation and device security (designed to specify and enforce proper access to and use of workstations where PHI can be accessed at a healthcare facility).

The third and final category is technical safeguards. Generally, technical safeguards are steps your practice takes to insulate PHI in your possession from electronic threats. Technical safeguards include but again are not limited to: 1) access controls (designed to ensure only authorized personnel access PHI); 2) audit controls, (designed to record and examine access and other activity in information systems containing PHI); 3) integrity controls (designed to ensure PHI is not improperly altered or destroyed); and 4) transmission controls (designed to guard against unauthorized use of seizure of PHI transmitted over an electronic network).

While virtually every practitioner with whom I have spoken has at least a working familiarity with the HIPAA privacy rule, I never cease to be amazed by how few practitioners understand even the basics of the HIPAA security rule. Both rules have been in place for the same amount of time. A violation of the HIPAA security rule is no less a HIPAA violation than a violation of the privacy rule. Violations of either rule can result in very significant monetary penalties and as of 2010 can also result in criminal penalties under certain extreme circumstances.

In the 21st century the days of Polaroid cameras and film negatives are far in the past. Virtually all photography conducted in the clinical setting is now done digitally. This brings into play the more recent companion statute to the HIPAA laws, the Health Information Technology for Economic and Clinical Health (HITECH) Act. The primary purpose of the HITECH Act was to encourage the adoption of electronic medical records (EMRs) by providing both financial incentives for their adoption and financial penalties for the failure to transition to EMR systems. However, HITECH also contains a subpart dealing with the improper and/or inadvertent disclosure of electronic PHI that is applicable to digital photography.

Under the HITECH Act, clinical providers who engage in digital photography must take reasonable steps to avoid breaches of their digitally stored PHI, including digital photographs. Most unauthorized uses or disclosures of digital PHI can constitute HITECH breaches. However, a specific exception is made for the inadvertent disclosure of electronic PHI (in photographic form or otherwise) by one practitioner to another practitioner in the same institution. Thus, the simple fact that one provider who is not caring for a particular patient happens to view a photograph of that patient containing PHI in an institutional healthcare setting does not, in and of itself, constitute a HITECH breach.

When a HITECH breach occurs, the practitioner whose photographs (or other electronic PHI) have been improperly accessed must take steps to rectify the situation or face penalties. The most important step is commonly to notify all patients whose electronic PHI may have been compromised by the breach. There are strict statutory requirements for what constitutes proper breach notification. These vary depending on the nature of the electronic PHI involved and the magnitude of the breach itself. Encryption of PHI, including photographs, is one recognized way to avoid a breach, as the unauthorized use or disclosure of encrypted PHI does not constitute a breach under the statute itself. However, most if not all digital cameras are not capable of encrypting photographs taken. For this reason, at the present time, there is little or no effective technological way to prevent photographic breaches through encryption at least until the point when the photographs are transferred from the digital camera to a depository where encryption is possible.

Furthermore, in my experience, a disturbingly high percentage of institutions allow personal photographic devices (sometimes even including camera phones) to be used by employees and/or medical staff members for clinical photography. Even when the photography itself is performed in an appropriate setting and by an appropriate practitioner, the use of such personal devices creates inherent and unnecessary legal risks. There is little most institutions can do to properly meet their HIPAA security and HITECH security requirements with respect to personal photographic devices owned by their employees or medical staff. The simple fact that employees often take home these devices when their shift ends, often with electronic PHI continuing to reside in their memory cards, in and of itself constitutes a significant and avoidable risk. For this reason, one of the most basic and most important preventative legal steps you can take with respect to photography is to provide institutional cameras to your employees who take clinical photographs, and insist that those cameras be used only for that purpose and only in your facility itself. Establishing a secure central depository for electronic photographs after they are taken, ideally one with encryption capability, is also a prudent preventative legal care move.

"Even when the photography itself is performed in an appropriate setting and by an appropriate practitioner, the use of personal devices creates inherent and unnecessary legal risks."

There are also medical-legal issues relating to photography in the healthcare setting unrelated to clinical photographs taken by clinical practitioners. Now that camera phones are almost ubiquitous, virtually any patient or patient's family member will have the technological capability of taking photographs anywhere in a clinical healthcare institution. However, the mere fact that patients and their families have the ability to take such photographs does not necessarily give them the legal right to do so. Although the patient is the master of his or her own body and healthcare, the facility itself remains private property. The owner and/or the operator of the facility has the right to restrict otherwise legal activity on its premises. This can include restrictions on patient photography if the institution desires to implement them.

Many specialized healthcare institutions already enforce very strict limits on patient and family photography. Psychiatric institutions and substance-abuse centers, for example, very often enforce a blanket prohibition on such photography, basing it on the privacy needs of not only their patients but also their staff. These same justifications can apply to any healthcare facility and any type of healthcare practice. Establishing an institutional policy prohibiting the taking of all photographs other than those taken by practitioners for clinical purposes is, in my opinion, a worthwhile preventative legal step. After it is enacted, the policy should be widely posted and politely but firmly enforced. While this will not prevent all patients from taking photographs inside a clinical facility, it undoubtedly will help to one extent or the other, and it will certainly cause no harm.

Finally, in today's modern visual society, photographs are often the single most powerful evidence in medical legal litigation. A picture is quite literally worth more than a thousand words in a medical record when it comes to persuading a jury. When evaluating and prospectively managing the litigation risks of clinical photographs, the essential preventative legal consideration for practitioners is the question of control.

Clinical photographs themselves are neither inherently helpful nor inherently dangerous from a medical-legal perspective. In fact, photographs often validate either the memory of healthcare practitioners regarding a patient's condition or the clinical decisions they may make. Furthermore, the absence of a photograph where one is either clinically or legally expected can be just as legally damaging as a photograph that contradicts an assumption made as part of the clinical decision-making process.

The single best way to manage the medical-legal risks of photography in the litigation arena is to prospectively establish controls over photography in your institution or your practice. Careful prospective consideration of questions, such as: 1) when will photography be allowed (or required), 2) who will be allowed to conduct photography, 3) what devices will be allowed (or required) to be used for photography, and 4) what devices will be allowed (or again required) to store photographs once taken, will go a long way to ensuring that whatever your policy on photography may be, it maximizes the benefits to your patients while minimizing the avoidable legal risks to you and your institution.

CHAPTER 8

Transparency and Confidentiality

One of the most important initiatives in healthcare today from a medical-legal standpoint is the ongoing movement toward transparency. It is also one of the most fundamental changes in how the healthcare industry approaches adverse events and the potential liability they bring that has been experienced in years. Across the country, institutions ranging from large hospital networks to private practices are embracing the idea that transparency in the face of adverse events is beneficial to both the practitioner and the patient. Many factors are driving this truly revolutionary change.

First, there is a growing consensus in healthcare that transparency in the face of adverse events leads to higher quality care. Transparency, it is claimed, results in more thorough, accurate, and effective investigations into adverse events. Transparency is also claimed to lead to better and more comprehensive quality-improvement measures being implemented after unfortunate events occur. To the extent these assumptions are true, patients undeniably benefit from transparency in the investigative process. Moreover, more and more institutions are concluding that their own staff members benefit from the empowerment that comes from widespread transparent disclosure not only of adverse events but also of the steps an institution is taking to prevent the occurrence of similar events in the future.

Finally, the undeniable movement toward linking reimbursement to the quality of care provided is also a driving force behind transparency for many institutions. As quality of care becomes an ever more important criteria for reimbursement, the fiscal reality that it creates will make transparency an imperative for virtually all healthcare providers regardless of their beliefs regarding its efficacy in promoting better responses to adverse events and overall better care.

It is important for all healthcare providers contemplating a transparency initiative to remember and understand two important facts from the outset. First, transparency is not a point-in-place goal that is either obtained or missed. Unlike sterility in the operating-room setting, transparency is never either wholly present or absent. To the contrary, transparency is better viewed as a linear process. It can and should be achieved to varying degrees for varying circumstances. Accordingly, approaching any transparency initiative with a "one size fits all" mentality is likely to lead to both unnecessary inefficiencies and unforeseen complications.

Second, it is important to recognize that transparency is inherently and conversely linked to another equally important consideration: control. Every move to increase transparency by definition decreases control over the information being disclosed. In fact, it is no exaggeration to say that the concept of transparency cannot be accurately understood or discussed without a simultaneous consideration of the control issue. Like the concepts of heaven and hell, an accurate understanding of one requires a consideration of the other.

The control question with respect to data relating to adverse events generally centers on issues relating to hospital and medical peer-review committee privileges. These privileges, codified in federal law as well as in the law of virtually every state, provide powerful and sometimes almost unbreakable shields to healthcare providers when evaluating quality-of-care issues. Further, the scope of the privilege protections these statutes provide is, in most cases, almost unbelievably broad. In many jurisdictions confidentiality statutes protect not only the credentialing of healthcare providers but also the investigation of specific adverse events. Even general nonspecific inquiries into the overall quality of care provided at an institution, unrelated to particular patients or events, can often be controlled through the application of these privileges. Incredibly, many healthcare professionals do not fully recognize the extent to which these confidentiality statutes provide them with almost absolute control over their quality-of-care initiatives should they choose to avail themselves of those protections.

At their heart, transparency initiatives involve critical decision-making regarding the appropriate balance between the two competing and mutually exclusive goals of transparency and control. From a practical standpoint, they therefore often involve difficult decisions regarding the extent, if any, to which an institution should voluntarily choose not to avail itself of the confidentiality protections afforded it by the statutes of its jurisdiction. It is critical for healthcare providers to recognize at the onset that the decision to remove a particular investigation or quality initiative from the committee process that would otherwise guarantee it confidentiality is often an irrevocable one. During the course of an investigation, once the statutory formalities for claiming a hospital or medical peer-review committee privilege have been varied from, it can be very difficult, if not impossible, to regain control over that investigation if it is later decided that transparency in that particular instance is either ill-advised or inappropriate.

When considerations of the appropriate balance between control and transparency are not undertaken before a transparency initiative is rolled out, unforeseen and unfortunate complications may result. An example of this recently occurred at a tertiary care hospital client of mine. In the interest of furthering transparency with its own employees, the hospital decided to post detailed information on the number and nature of patient injury events in its facility on its internal intranet website. The laudable and limited purpose for this disclosure was to educate hospital staff regarding the types of events that were unfortunately occurring and what was hoped to be the demonstrable trend in reducing them. Because the disclosure was made on an internal computer system accessible only by hospital employees, the implications with respect to overall control of the information were not fully considered. Much to the surprise of the hospital officials in charge of the project, the information posted internally was soon released in a far more public fashion. Not surprisingly, this release led to negative publicity for the facility, an unwanted and unfortunate side effect that was not fully appreciated by senior hospital management before the initiative was set in motion. Had more thought been given to the loss of control implications of this idea at higher levels before it was approved, a better mechanism for achieving essentially the same transparency goals could likely have been identified and enacted. In this particular case, by the time that complication was recognized, the damage had been done.

For the reasons outlined above, the best transparency initiatives contain the following components. First, effective transparency initiatives are always implemented at the highest decision-making level and only after careful consideration of the appropriate balance between transparency and control for the individual institution involved. Because the dangers associated with the necessary loss of control implicit in any transparency initiative are so significant, only the highest levels of institutional management should authorize any significant movement toward transparency. Similarly, to achieve the laudable goals they can potentially advance, transparency initiatives must be consistently applied throughout an institution. Only approval and implementation of a transparency initiative at the highest management level can ensure such consistency takes place.

Second, transparency initiatives should be carefully tailored to work as closely as possible in tandem with existing control mechanisms, including hospital and medical peer-review committee privileges. Careful consideration should be given to the question of how a transparency initiative will impact existing committee structures and the privileges they can provide when properly utilized. If a transparency initiative will compromise the ability of a committee to perform its existing functions, it is important that the members of that committee are educated regarding the transparency initiative before it is implemented. A failure to do so will almost inevitably lead to unforeseen and potentially dangerous complications for the healthcare institutions when it is faced with its next serious adverse event or other occurrence that falls in the purview of both the transparency initiative and the existing committee investigative structure.

> *"In a well-functioning transparency initiative, the final decision on transparent disclosure of any critical or sensitive information should always be one of the final decisions reached."*

Third, to the greatest extent possible an institution's transparency initiatives should maintain the institution's ability to exercise control over data when circumstances exist that justify a variance from any standard transparency policy. The best approach toward this goal, in my opinion, is to design a transparency initiative that operates via a mechanism for the removal of otherwise confidential and controlled data from the committee structure for its transparent release. The opposite approach — gathering such sensitive information and data entirely outside of the protective sphere created by a committee structure — is ill-advised.

It is important to keep in mind that the privileges that provide legal confidentiality for the investigations of adverse events and quality-of-care issues are best viewed as safety nets for your protection as you cross the tightrope of a sensitive investigation. Once you have crossed that tightrope, you are free to do whatever you wish, including full transparent disclosure of all of the information gathered and conclusions reached as part of the process. But there is no reason to remove the safety net and walk the tightrope in a far more dangerous fashion simply because, at the end of the line, you have decided to do something different with the information obtained, either in the interest of transparency or otherwise.

Put another way, it is important to remember that privileges can always be waived. However, it is equally important to remember that once they are waived they are very difficult if not impossible to reclaim. In a well-functioning transparency initiative, the ultimate and often irrevocable decision on transparent disclosure of any critical or sensitive information should always be one of the final decisions reached. Protecting yourself and your institution with the safety net of privilege until the time when the final decision on transparency is made diminishes neither the ultimate transparency provided nor the benefits from that transparency itself. It merely makes the process of arriving at the appropriately balanced position between transparency and control far safer for both the institution itself and all of the individual practitioners involved.

In summary, transparency is a very laudable goal with much to recommend for both patients and healthcare providers. However, the manner in which you approach the process leading up to transparency can have a significant impact on the real-world implications of the process itself. Recognizing the control issues implicit in any transparency initiative upfront and designing your transparency process to minimize its unavoidable diminution of your institutional control of sensitive data will allow you to maximize the advantages from transparency while minimizing its inherit risks.

CHAPTER 9

Criminal Law Issues

When senior practitioners reminisce about the medical-legal landscape of ten or twenty years ago, they often do so with little nostalgia for the days before tort reform, when the perceived exposure to civil liability most medical practitioners faced was, almost without question, significantly greater than it is today. However, those 20th-century practitioners enjoyed one significant medical-legal benefit that clinicians today do not enjoy, even with all the benefits of tort reform. Specifically, those earlier practitioners did not have to face nearly the substantial risk of medical-legal exposure in the criminal arena that 21st-century practitioners face but often fail to recognize.

In this day and age, criminal liability is a real risk for both individual and institutional healthcare practitioners across the country. High-profile cases such as Dr. Conrad Murray's conviction for manslaughter in connection with the death of Michael Jackson garner the headlines. However, it is the slow yet steady encroachment of criminal law into the realm of medical practice that should be the true focus of concern on this issue.

One need only look in detail at Dr. Murray's criminal trial to see a clear example of how much overlap presently exists between criminal and civil law in the area of medical liability. Dr. Murray was found guilty of involuntary manslaughter. Under California law, involuntary manslaughter is the commission of a lawful act but with criminal negligence and/or the failure to perform a legal duty that results in criminal negligence. To establish these essential elements, however, prosecutors made a very medically specific argument. In their case in chief and in their closing arguments, the prosecutors successfully convinced the jury that Dr. Murray was criminally negligent by varying significantly from acceptable medical practices in four specific areas: choosing to administer Propofol to Mr. Jackson; failing to have proper monitoring equipment once Propofol was administered; failing to call 911 immediately after Mr. Jackson began experiencing complications; and failing to keep proper records of his use of Propofol in Mr. Jackson's care.

The incredible similarity between the factual specifics of the criminal case against Dr. Murray and the factual specifics of hundreds of medical-malpractice cases brought against anesthesiologists across the country is striking. In my judgment, any or all of the allegations that were made against Dr. Murray and used to incarcerate him could have just as easily been made in a civil lawsuit against Dr. Murray by Mr. Jackson's estate. Put another way, the same evidence and allegations that once subjected practitioners only to monetary liability in the civil court system can now be used, in and of themselves, to subject those same practitioners to criminal convictions and potential incarceration.

The reasons for the expansion of criminal liability into the medical-legal arena are numerous. First and foremost, the encroachment of criminal law into the medical sphere is simply an example of the trend toward criminalization of conduct that has been quietly ongoing in American society for decades. Second, the advent of courtroom reality shows and lucrative legal commentary positions on specialty news stations has created powerful incentives for the prosecution of high-profile defendants in high-profile cases. The patient involved in the medical death does not have to be as famous as Michael Jackson for an unexpected and serious medical complication to meet these criteria. Because 21st-century prosecutors are now sometimes expected to prosecute "bad" medical conduct (by the media if no one else), these types of prosecutions have increased and are likely to continue to increase in the future.

"The same evidence and allegations that once subjected practitioners only to monetary liability in the civil court system can now be used to subject those same practitioners to criminal convictions and potential incarceration."

In some cases prosecutions are also initiated based on poorly worded or simply vague criminal statutes. In many cases, it is almost impossible to distinguish between the type of conduct that will statutorily result in civil liability and the type of conduct that can statutorily result in imprisonment under criminal law. Consider this comparison of the following two statutes. When reading them, try to identify the one that, when violated, could subject a practitioner to criminal liability and potentially incarceration. One statute carries such a risk, while the other one does not.

Statute No. 1: Liability exists when *a person acts in a reckless way that causes a high risk of death or great bodily injury and a reasonable person would have known that acting in that way would create such a risk.*

Statute No. 2: Liability exists when *a person acts, and from his or her standpoint the act at the time of its occurrence involves an extreme degree of risk, considering the probability and magnitude of the potential harm to others, and the person has actual subjective awareness of the risk involved but nevertheless proceeds with conscious indifference to the rights, safety, or welfare of others.*

The first statute listed above is the California definition of criminal negligence, the statutory provision under which Dr. Conrad Murray was convicted and incarcerated. The second statute is the Texas civil-law definition of malice, under which exemplary damages are recoverable in the Texas civil-liability system. Even if you successfully guessed which statute was the criminal one and which was the civil one on at first glance, it is hard not to recognize the extreme similarity between the legal standards established by these two statutory provisions. As long as the evidentiary and legal standard for criminal liability is this close to the standard for civil liability, the possibility of encroachment by criminal law into the medical-legal arena will always remain a very real risk.

Although it is dangerous to generalize, for the most part criminal risk in the medical-legal context is centered on certain groups and certain types of conduct. With respect to patient groups, the statutory authority for criminal prosecution of healthcare providers is most often found in statutes designed to protect particularly vulnerable members of the population: e.g., the elderly, the significantly infirm, and the very young. The type of conduct that is most often criminalized is not simple medical negligence (Dr. Conrad Murray's case notwithstanding); rather, it is typically conduct that can be categorized as either abuse, neglect, or mistreatment of a vulnerable individual.

Criminal risk is also no longer limited to the clinical care context. In today's medical-legal environment, criminal risks exist in connection with many of the administrative functions associated with a modern medical practice. More and more the federal government, as the principle payor for the medical services, is looking upon sometimes innocent billing mistakes as potential criminal acts. Criminal prosecutions of healthcare institutions and individual practitioners for alleged fraudulent Medicare and Medicaid billing, as well as false claims under the federal False Claims Act, have increased significantly over the past decade. There are reasons to believe they will continue to increase over the next few decades as well.

It is also important to remember that, unlike many civil plaintiffs' attorneys, some criminal prosecutors have little or no more medical expertise than ordinary laymen. The unquestioned medical expertise of many civil plaintiffs' attorneys, developed over years of pursuing legitimate healthcare liability claims on behalf of injured patients, often works to the (sometimes unintended) advantage of practitioners. It allows experienced civil plaintiff's attorneys to accurately judge the medical merits of civil claims at a very early stage in the civil justice process. Lacking that same level of medical experience and medical expertise, some prosecutors erroneously see potential criminal liability under medical facts and/or circumstances which would not strike a seasoned civil attorney as actionable.

Unlike the civil-liability system, once a criminal investigation has been initiated against a practitioner, that practitioner is already ensured of enormous financial and personal risk. This is true even if the criminal investigation never proceeds far enough to put the practitioner at the most serious of all risks; the loss of liberty as the result of incarceration. First, in most if not all jurisdictions, no practitioner can insure himself or herself against criminal risk. From a practical standpoint, this means that there is no mechanism by which a third party can be obligated to pay the legal expenses associated with a criminal defense. Put simply, if you as a medical practitioner need a criminal-defense lawyer, you as a medical practitioner will have to pay for a lawyer. This cost can easily run into the tens of thousands of dollars even if a criminal investigation does not lead to a full trial.

Additionally, medical and nursing licensing bodies are not required to wait for finality from the criminal justice system before taking action. In fact, many would argue (and some licensing boards would agree) that the critical priority of protecting the public demands that boards not wait for technical legal finalities before taking action against accused practitioners. Thus, any practitioner facing a criminal investigation, even a very preliminary one, also runs a high risk of simultaneously facing a thorough inquiry from his or her licensing body. That means that the only relatively less significant risk of loss of professional standing often accompanies the risk of incarceration for practitioners involved with the criminal justice system.

Further, once a criminal investigation is started, the chances that the case will proceed to a scheduled trial are high. Most of the preliminary mechanisms involved in the criminal investigative process are weighted heavily toward the prosecution. In other words, it is often easy in most states and in most cases for a prosecutor to gain an indictment and therefore gain the right to go to trial against virtually any defendant he or she wishes to pursue. And once that prosecutor obtains the right to proceed to a jury trial, he or she has incredibly significant leverage to force a plea agreement in a criminal case.

What does a criminal defendant risk when he or she elects to go to trial rather than accept a plea bargain? First and foremost is the real possibility of lengthy incarceration. However, as mentioned above, professional licenses as well as personal finances are also almost always at risk. Many practitioners, just like many other defendants, will find the pressure to accept a plea to a lesser criminal charge almost irresistible, especially if that plea agreement does not necessitate a forfeiture of a professional license and a lifetime career in medicine.

To manage this type of risk, 21st-century practitioners must learn the criminal law governing the jurisdiction in which they practice. It is of particular importance for practitioners to know the legal definitions of abuse and neglect as they are defined in their jurisdiction's criminal code. It is no longer sufficient to simply have a rudimentary knowledge of civil-liability law and rely on your institution's risk manager or your insurance adjuster to guide you through the specifics of potential civil liability when an adverse event occurs. It is also incumbent upon practitioners to understand how their medical records can be a source of increased criminal legal risk in today's climate. Like a plaintiff's personal-injury attorney, the first information that a prosecutor is likely to look at when investigating a criminal complaint is the patient's medical records. If documentation in the records, or the lack thereof, suggests abuse or neglect as those terms are defined under a state's criminal law statutes, the prosecutor is highly likely to initiate a criminal investigation.

Practitioners also need to recognize up front that there is no such thing as an "informal" or "unimportant" criminal investigation. Any time someone from the criminal justice system seeks information from a practitioner about his or her care of a patient, it absolutely must be approached with deadly earnest. Even if he or she resides in a small or rural jurisdiction where the local prosecutor is a neighbor or a friend, in my professional opinion, no practitioner should ever voluntarily participate in a criminal investigation into his or her care without the prior advice and assistance of good criminal legal counsel. Even if a practitioner is assured that a question or inquiry is "off the record," "routine" or "necessary to avoid a real inquiry" this cardinal rule still holds true.

Accordingly, like the computer Joshua said in the 1983 movie *WarGames*, the only winning move in the criminal-justice game is not to play. If you (or more accurately your criminal defense counsel—never negotiate alone) cannot successfully convince a prosecutor not to actively pursue a case that might draw his or her initial interest, you are faced with a losing proposition, and the only remaining question is the degree of loss.

Sadly, criminal liability for medical conduct, both in the clinical setting and outside of the patient room, is a reality all 21st-century practitioners face. Those practitioners who do not take the time to understand how criminal law applies to their practice and to adjust their documentation, reimbursement and reporting routines accordingly are failing to apply preventative legal care principles to one of the single greatest areas of risk they face today.

CHAPTER 10
Conclusions

At the risk of giving away secrets vital to the continuing financial success of my chosen profession, it is not an exaggeration to say that many of the problems that cause healthcare providers to engage defense counsel are, in large part, mostly preventable ones. Some stem from pervasive and self-injurious misunderstandings of the true nature of the medical-legal process. Others arise from the simple failure to consider the medical-legal implications of entirely admirable and worthwhile clinical care initiatives. Still others find their genesis in what can only be called a simple and, to my mind, inexcusable lack of concern on the part of healthcare providers and institutions for maintaining their legal health in the absence of acute, critical events and circumstances.

This book was designed to be a simple road map to rectify many of these problems and thereby avoid many of their consequences going forward. It is based on my sincere belief, based on over 20 years of experience, that if healthcare practitioners would spend half of the time prospectively managing their medical-legal issues that they spend constantly imploring their patients to spend prospectively managing their health issues that those legal issues would decrease in both their frequency and severity to an extent that would almost defy belief.

Few of the recommendations outlined in this book can truly be characterized as either cutting-edge innovations or brilliant new strategies. Similarly, even fewer of the ideas expressed herein arise to the level of deep thoughts or "rocket science." For the most part, I honestly believe they can most accurately be characterized as common-sense solutions to what are relatively straightforward problems at their core. What I hope this means for the reader is that there is nothing contained in this book that cannot be implemented in his or her healthcare practice with nothing more than a little diligent effort. By way of candid self-disclosure, I also believe that almost every suggestion contained in this book can be implemented without incurring substantial legal expense in the process. It is my firm belief and sincere hope that all readers agree with these assessments.

A general surgeon who is a friend of mine from Houston is fond of saying there are two types of physicians in America: those who have been involved in litigation and those who will be involved in litigation. That may or may not be true. What is beyond dispute, however, is that there are no true winners among the universe of healthcare providers who find themselves involuntarily entangled in the legal system. Even those who ultimately prevail either by adjudication, jury verdict or otherwise are, in a true sense, losers as well. The only real question is one of degree.

Even the successful subgroup of healthcare litigants, the ones who are ultimately completely exonerated, incur significant expense working their way through the legal process. More important, even that entirely successful subgroup has been forced to devote often significant amounts of time, energy, and attention that otherwise could have been more profitably focused on their patients and their profession. Those healthcare providers who find themselves facing an adverse judgment of some kind at the end of the medical-legal road lose on an entirely different level and in an entirely different way. Perhaps even more important, among those healthcare practitioners who are not entirely successful in their defense of medical legal accusations are a subgroup who find the medical-legal experience so unpleasant and upsetting that they either change their practice in a detrimental defensive way or stop providing certain aspects of clinical care altogether. When such unfortunate medical-legal complications arise, it is often not just the practitioner but also society as a whole that loses in the process. Once again, for all the reasons cited herein, to my mind the only winning move is not to play.

Medical-legal consequences arising from negligent patient care are neither unjustified nor properly avoidable. Nothing in this book or any other book on this topic should suggest otherwise. It is, however, an unfortunate fact that maximizing the quality of healthcare you provide will only go so far in terms of minimizing the medical-legal complications your clinical practice will encounter.

Nothing in this book is intended as a substitute for the best possible care of your patients. Nothing in this book is intended to supersede the goal of providing the best possible care to your patients. What this book is designed to do is suggest simple, straightforward and workable ways for healthcare practitioners to complement their quality of care efforts with an effective prospective approach to medical-legal risk management. By doing so, it is my hope and honest expectation that practitioners will minimize their chances of ensnarement in the legal system for reasons wholly unrelated to the clinical care they provide.

I hope all my readers find this book to be a useful resource in their on-going efforts to provide the best care they can to their patients. And I hope all readers find successful solutions in its pages that allow them to complement the excellent clinical care they provide to their patients with at least an ounce of preventative legal care for themselves.

ABOUT THE AUTHOR

Kevin W. Yankowsky is a partner in the Life Sciences Pharmaceutical and Health Litigation Practice Group of Norton Rose Fulbright US LLP. Kevin has served as lead counsel for healthcare industry defendants in over 30 jury trials and 12 appeals in both state and federal court, the majority of which involved claimed damages at trial in excess of $1 million. Kevin's trial practice encompasses virtually all types of civil litigation facing the healthcare industry. He serves as lead counsel in professional liability claims, complex commercial suits, products liability matters, ERISA actions, premises liability suits and EMTALA litigation and regulatory investigations. In addition to his extensive courtroom experience, Kevin advises clients on Joint Commission investigations, patient privacy, data retention and security issues, and hospital committee and medical peer review matters. Kevin also serves as a frequent consultant on legal, litigation, document retention, electronic data management, and enterprise risk issues for health industry clients. Kevin's established reputation as both an accomplished trial lawyer and risk management consultant have also made him a frequently featured speaker at national healthcare industry conferences and professional symposiums across the country.

Printed in the USA
CPSIA information can be obtained
at www.ICGtesting.com
LVHW010332280824
789294LV00004B/112

9 781930 536777